MW01092613

A
SHORT
GUIDE
TO

CHURCH

A
SHORT
GUIDE
TO

CHURCH

A
SHORT
GUIDE
TO

CHURCH

What Is It All About?

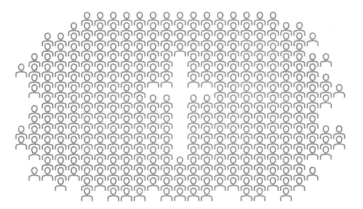

DEAN INSERRA

PUBLISHING
BRENTWOOD, TENNESSEE

Published by B&H Publishing Group
Brentwood, Tennessee

Dewey Decimal Classification: 254.5
Subject Heading: CHURCH / DISCIPLESHIP
/ CHURCH MEMBERSHIP

Cover design by Darren Welch Design.
Illustration by Peacefully7/shutterstock.
Author photo by City Church staff.

1 2 3 4 5 6 • 27 26 25 24

To Alex Scott and Ashlyn Portero.
Thank you for loving the local church.

Acknowledgments

I CANNOT WRITE A book about the local church without thanking City Church of Tallahassee, for being the home church of my family, and a place we love. It truly is the dearest place. Thank you for being a church we would want to be members of even if I wasn't on the staff. We love our church.

I would also like to thank Giana Hall for always being the first person who sees my writing and a trusted and gifted friend.

I am grateful for Erik Wolgemuth at Wolgemuth and Associates, and B&H Publishing Group for giving me this opportunity, along with my guide throughout the process, Logan Pyron.

Finally, I would like thank the Elders and Executive Staff at City Church for being the trusted leadership we need to flourish.

Contents

Foreword

I GREW UP AS an only child of divorced parents. I was deeply loved by my parents, but I didn't really grow up around family. No grandparents, no siblings, no aunts, or uncles. I also didn't really grow up in the church, nor did I have an understanding of the gospel. Our family rhythms were centered around work, sports, and school.

I was in college when I first heard the gospel presented to me. Someone sat down with me in the university student center and presented a gospel tract to me. He shared with me that God made me, that I was living in rebellion to him, that Jesus paid the price for my sin, and that I could have everlasting life with him by placing my faith in Christ. Through the work of the Holy Spirit, God used this simple gospel message to transfer me from the kingdom of darkness to the kingdom of his Son. I was dead, but God made me alive.

I spent the next several years very engaged in campus ministry. My parents once said it felt like I was majoring in ministry and minoring in college. During those years, I learned how to share my faith. I spent time in Christian community and grew in my love for the Lord. These were really sweet years for me, but one thing I never really understood was the church. What is a church for when I have what I need in campus ministry? Is the church *really* necessary? During those years, I was growing in Christ, but I was separated from his body. In fact, where I pastor now, by far the greatest area of confusion for confessing Christians is the church.

Over the last several decades evangelicals have attempted to center the gospel in all that we do. This gospel-centered movement has rightly emphasized the holiness of God, the sinfulness of humanity, the sacrificial and atoning work of Christ, and the indwelling presence of the Holy Spirit. But what about the church?

Throughout the past fifteen years, my understanding of the gospel has grown wider and deeper. More specifically, I understand that being adopted into the family of God, the church, is part of the gospel. The good news of the gospel is not just that we are saved from something, the judgment of God, but that we're also saved into something—the family of God. Entrance into this new family should be good news for all Christians. For all of us who are lonely, outcasts, spiritual or physical orphans, or to anyone looking for a family, the church is good news. God has not just saved us from hell, he has adopted us into his family.

The church is good news, because when we are saved into this family, we stand on God's Word together. We are full of the Holy Spirit together. We pray together. We sing together. We encourage one another together. We invite sinners to repentance, belief, and baptism together. We enjoy the Lord's Supper together. And we will, one day, enjoy a kingdom without end together.

I am thankful you've picked up this book about the church, but you may still be asking the question, "Why does the church matter?" It is because the gospel matters.

—J. T. English, pastor, professor, author of *Deep Discipleship* and coauthor of *You Are a Theologian*

CHAPTER 1

What's the Deal with Church? Do I Have to Go?

THERE IS MORE TO being a Christian than going to church, but there is certainly not less. The local church is significant in the lives of those who follow Jesus Christ, whether through its presence or its absence. Of all the pushback I get on social media from professing Christians, the most consistent negative comments come when I assert what I thought was a basic understanding: Christians should go to church. The rebuttal is predictable, almost automatic: "You don't have to go to church to be a Christian." And, of course, church attendance does not forgive sins or reconcile anyone to God. It is by grace we have been saved, through faith, not by works (Eph. 2:8–9). We are forgiven and saved from God's just punishment of sin through the substitutionary death of Jesus Christ. One does not have to go to church or do any other work whatsoever to be saved, since Jesus has done all the work through his perfect life, death on the cross, and glorious resurrection.

The New Testament is full of inferences and references to the role of the church in the life of a believer. The professing Christian who does not go to church will say that one can "have church"—on a boat, playing golf, sitting on the back porch enjoying a Sunday morning coffee. "It is about your personal relationship with God." While I want to acknowledge that these individuals may have been taught that at some time in their lives or been convinced of it by a friend, Scripture just does not recognize an unchurched Christianity. Yes, we can have a personal experience with God anywhere in creation, but that is not the ultimate point regarding the Christian and the church. The better option is to discover and pursue what God has *willed* and *designed* for his people to live out the Christian life and experience.

Throughout the New Testament, God's design for his people is the church. Outside of an important instruction from the writer of Hebrews for the Christians not to neglect gathering together (Heb. 10:25), you may not think there are an abundant number of slam-dunk, drop-the-hammer, case-closed commandments about the Christian being part of the church. However, the letters of the New Testament are written in the assumed context of local church congregations. If I am telling you about the game Tom Brady played where he threw touchdown passes, I don't also have to inform you that he's playing football. The context is the football game. Similarly, the Holy Spirit-inspired New Testament letters are addressed to actual churches. Local churches are the context.

The claim that "we *are* the church; we don't *go to* church" sounds spiritual (and is not completely wrong), but there is much scriptural emphasis on the local church, perhaps even more than the universal church. The New Testament letters were written to actual, organized churches that existed at the time. This is the context for living out the new life to which we are called. Jonathan Leeman wrote that "membership in the universal church must become visible in a local gathering of Christians."[1]

The New Testament letters were written to actual, organized churches that existed at the time.

As a pastor, I officiate weddings on a regular basis. I count it as a privilege to be asked by a couple to stand with them on their wedding day, share the Scriptures concerning marriage, lead them in their vows, and pronounce them husband and wife. My relationship with the couple is certainly a major reason officiating is meaningful, but there is an even greater reason. I am getting to take part in God's model for his church: a husband loving his wife as Christ loved the church.

At the beginning of the ceremony, after I welcome the guests on behalf of the bride and the groom, I remind the wedding guests that they did not simply fill out an RSVP form and choose chicken, beef, or vegetarian for their meal at the reception. They are not merely spectators. By attending this wedding, they are witnesses to God's grand design, affirming that they approve what is taking place. The bride and groom are participating in what God has made, and the guests get to affirm this grand plan.

Another grand design for God's people is the church. I believe Christians should see local church membership as the great privilege of getting to take part in and belong to the design God has given specifically, uniquely, and specially for his children, his people. Unfortunately, many who claim the title of Christian do not embrace this design. Data from a study conducted by Christian researcher Ryan Burge finds that

> the number of self-identified evangelicals who attend church regularly continues to drop, with 26.7 percent saying they seldom or never go to church. About 13.5 percent of self-identified evangelicals say they go to church "yearly," bringing the number of

evangelicals who go to church once a year or less to about 40.2 percent. About half of self-identified evangelicals attend weekly or more, with the other 10 percent saying they attend about once a month.[2]

Making the church a priority in the lives of Christians is dwindling, and even nonexistent for some. Yes, church is somewhere we physically go, but much more, it is something to which we belong as members of the body of Christ. Our membership in the body of Christ is universal, applying to believers throughout history, across the world, past, present, and future, and it is expressed locally through specific congregations. To be a Christian and not have the church as a significant part of one's life is either to deny or neglect God's design. It is not an exaggeration, then, to call the trend of an unchurched Christianity a crisis. But before we dive into an overview of what the church is and what it does, I want to cover some potential reasons the unchurched Christian is a reality.

Yes, church is somewhere we physically go, but much more, it is something to which we belong as members of the body of Christ.

UNCHURCHED CHRISTIAN

Some have not been told.

After first coming to faith in Christ, I went all the way through my teenage years without anyone teaching me about the significance of the local church in the life of the believer. I thought it was just something you did on Sundays with your family because that's what people do in the South. I believed the gospel and had converted to Christianity, but I received discipleship from a parachurch ministry. I thank God for that ministry and believe the Lord used it to put the gospel in front of me and allow me to grow in my faith as a young high school student, but it was not the local church. That does not make the parachurch ministry bad or wrong, but it wasn't the ultimate design for God's people to experience discipleship and community and be on mission together. Parachurches are a tool, a type of extra "hook in the water" for specifically focused evangelism that targets particular groups of people—in my case, student athletes. These organizations were never meant to be a substitute for the local church. I did not know the church was the plan of God for the spiritual forming and flourishing of his people, so my concern for it was minimal.

Far too many believers today are in a similar situation, perhaps without even realizing it. What changed the game for me was being taught (through the Scriptures as a college student at a Christian university) that there is not a category or context for an unchurched Christian in the Bible. I am convinced that one of the reasons we see an increasing unchurched Christianity around us is because people have not been discipled to have a biblical framework as to why church matters. This is first and foremost a discipleship issue. It is important that anyone with influence over the forming of Christian disciples needs to provide a healthy emphasis on the significance of the local church. People cannot know unless they are taught. I believe some are hesitant to teach it because it may feel legalistic or come across as fostering disunity among believers to suggest that the parachurch is insufficient. "We are all on the same team," one might suggest. And yes, Christians should seek unity as the big family of God, but that unity and family are to be expressed through local churches. So, if you are part of a ministry outside of a local church, please equip those under your care with the knowledge that finding and committing to a Bible-believing, gospel-preaching church is for their absolute good. Model it yourself!

I am convinced that one of the reasons
we see an increasing unchurched
Christianity around us is because people
have not been discipled to have a biblical
framework as to why church matters.

Some have been misled.

Growing up in the Christian subculture of the 1990s, my peers and I were regularly told that what mattered most was our personal relationship with Jesus. That was the emphasis of seemingly every sermon, testimony, Bible study, and Christian conversation. It was about you and Jesus. I am thankful that God invites us into a relationship with him, but looking back, I can see how my generation may have wound up believing church is not that important. It is normal to hear a professing Christian say, "I have my own relationship with God," or "the church isn't a building." Again, true. But we cannot forget that "the church is a people who gather together."[3] The New Testament letters are not addressed to random, isolated people in the first century having their personal moment with God out on a sheep pasture, but rather to Christians who were part of local churches. Many of those met under an actual roof, with established leaders, and a set time to meet for prayer, to hear the apostles' teachings, to take the Lord's Supper, and to sing spiritual songs together. To the person who has been taught that all that really matters is your personal relationship with Jesus, the author of Hebrews would remind you not to neglect gathering together, "as some are in the habit of doing, but encouraging each other, and all the more as you see the day approaching" (Heb. 10:25).

Do not be misled. The local church is essential. The church is understood as "we" significantly more than it is understood as simply about "me." People enter the Christian life as born-again individuals (John 3:3), but we live that life corporately as a community. The community we see in the Scriptures is centered around churches. The local church is the best thing going because it is God's idea. Jesus told his followers that he is the one building it (Matt. 16:18). How amazing it is to be part of that!

The church is understood as "we" significantly more than it is understood as simply about "me."

Some are out of the habit.

Every New Year I make a resolution that I am going to start being a "regular" at the gym. I am sure I am not alone in that. A friend who owns a fitness studio in my community told me they have more new clients at her gym in January than they do in the next six months combined. The gym only stays crowded with the new clientele for two to three weeks. Admittedly, and embarrassingly, I was one of the "two weekers" more Januarys than not. I had the best intentions, but I never got in the habit. I paid the fee for the special they were running, but never made it a priority in my life.

Then, one August, I realized that my health was important and that I needed some routine exercise. I signed up for three days a week with a trainer. I knew that every Monday, Tuesday, and Thursday I had a session at the gym at 8:00 a.m. It became not a matter of will or a New Year's resolution, but a scheduled part of my life. If it was important, it needed to become part of my routine. I knew when I went to sleep on Sunday night that I had the gym scheduled at 8:00 Monday morning. It became built into my week.

I do not know anyone who would discourage someone from establishing the healthy habit of a gym routine, so how much more important are our spiritual routines? Paul wrote: "The training of the body has limited benefit, but godliness is beneficial in every way, since it holds promise for the present life and also for the life to come" (1 Tim. 4:8). If habits are good for physical health, how much more important are they for our spiritual health? The reason some have lived an unchurched Christian life is not because they had a wrong understanding of the local church or had an improper theology; some just got out of the habit.

I post on my social media accounts on Saturday evenings that "Sunday morning church is a Saturday night decision." I type those words each week to help people remember that deciding you are going to church the next morning is a healthy habit. It is too easy to get out of the habit of doing anything. We must be intentional. Many churches saw much smaller numbers coming back after the COVID-19 pandemic (when many churches went months without meeting in person) than they had the week the doors shut at the start. Many people just established a new Sunday morning routine apart from the church. Some, frankly, have still not walked through the church doors since. When the writer of Hebrews encourages the believers to continue gathering together in chapter 10, he references those who had gotten out of the habit. They needed to be reminded again of the significance of the church. Those who had neglected the church did so because it became their "habit" (v. 25).

Some are stubborn.

"I'm a Christian, but I'm against organized religion." That is something I hear people claim far too often as they dig their heels into the ground. These are the people who adamantly claim that you do not have to go to church to be a Christian. It may even be the biggest conviction they hold out of all of their claimed "Christian" beliefs. Someone who holds this view may claim that he lives his life better than people he knows who go to church every week. He will usually point to a devotional he reads on his phone, insist he is a good person, and inform you that there is nothing in the Bible that says you must go to church. See reason number one for part of the problem.

Some had a negative experience.

It is important to err on the side of sensitivity and grace when it comes to those who claim to be Christians but no longer go to church because of what they have personally experienced on the inside. Sadly, in a sinful world full of brokenness, local churches are not exempt from ungodly behavior, mistreatment of others, selfish ambitions of leaders, and other troubling acts of ungodliness. But God's design is not the problem; sin is. Sinful behavior does not negate the truth that God has given us the church. Because some marriages sadly end in divorce does not mean the institution of marriage is the problem. Once again, sin is the problem.

My hope for those avoiding the church because of a past negative or hurtful experience is that they will realize they are missing a critical component of what it means to be a follower of Jesus and can prayerfully return with the intent to connect with a local church that seeks to honor Christ in unity. One can act out the gospel story of grace by forgiving the people Jesus died for and recover and pursue God's good design for their Christian life. As my friend Jared Wilson once posted on his social media: "If grace is real, you can begin again."[4]

Of course, the responsibility cannot rest solely on the victims here. Churches and church leaders need to actively offer resources to welcome and care for people who have experienced pain in church settings. We should keep in mind that people walking in our doors may have a wide range of experiences surrounding the church and for some it has not historically been a safe place. However the course of healing looks, the goal should be eventual belonging to a safe and biblical local church.

Some are not actual Christians.

Church can remain off the radar for some people because, by claiming to be a Christian in today's world, one can simply mean that he is a generic theist—meaning he is not an atheist, agnostic, or a member of another world religion. James states in his epistle: "You believe that God is one. Good! Even the demons believe—and they shudder" (James 2:19). Basic theism does not save one from their sins or bring one into the family of God. If one's answer to why he is a Christian does not depend on the work of Jesus Christ, he is most likely not a Christian (Matt. 7:21–23). The self-given label of *Christian* can be cultural rather than convictional, meaning it has nothing to do with what one believes about the gospel of Jesus Christ. Cultural Christianity exists inside the church, but is also a reason one who would write "Christian" on a form would also refuse to go to church. Why would they go to church if they have no real connection to Scripture or the gospel? It is nowhere on their life radar. The issue with the cultural Christian is not that they are unchurched, but rather that they are unconverted. More than simply getting to church, the cultural Christian needs to be saved.

Some have competing interests.

Many options in the world today compete for our attention, time, and loyalties. It is not uncommon to hear someone say they are just "too busy" to be regularly involved in church. If a family finally does have a Sunday off from travel, a prior commitment, or a kid's baseball tournament, they want to take a day to stay home, relax, and then get some things done. Whether errands, home improvement, or kids' schedules, there is always something that can win over going to church, let alone being committed to serving in one. Not too long ago, it would have been unheard of to have sports practices for kids on a Sunday, even outside of more traditionally religious areas of the country. But today, church is not even a factor in consideration when something is scheduled. This is the new reality for unchurched Christianity.

CONCLUSION

If you find yourself in one of the categories above or feel surrounded by people in your family, community, or even church body who fit in these categories, I pray that this book serves to ignite a passion for what the local church is designed to be. And if you are already enthusiastically serving the local church, I pray this book better equips you to answer the *why* for various elements of healthy church practice.

I believe in and love the local church and want to see everyone come to commit to and love it. This book aims to point us back to the beauty of God's clear design for his people that we call the local church. When that is established as a biblical conviction in the hearts and minds of believers, they get to enter the grand design God has gifted his people for his glory and our good. As Jesus builds his church, we get to join him in the amazing story of how God continues to gather and send his people, as he has designed them to function, and to flourish as those "for his possession, so that you may proclaim the praises of the one who called you out of darkness into his marvelous light" (1 Pet. 2:9).

DISCUSS AND REFLECT

1. Why is it not exactly true to claim "you don't go to church, you are the church." How has confusing that hurt people's view of the local church?

2. In your experience, what is the main reason professing Christians do not go to church?

3. What are the primary reasons the church should matter in the life of a Christian?

4. How does our individualistic society carry over to how some Christians view the church?

CHAPTER 2

Why Do We "Do" Church?

"I CAN DO IT myself!"

One day, my wife had an early-morning appointment, which meant it was my responsibility to get the kids ready and out the door for school. I love being a dad, but this set of tasks is not my strong suit, to say the least. At the time, my daughter was in kindergarten, so "getting the kids ready for school" involved getting her hair brushed and in a bow. Sadly, there was no dad college to teach me these skills. I grabbed her brush to tame her messy bedhead, and she quickly informed me that she was going to do it herself. (Somehow this does not happen when her mom gets her ready in the morning. But she was insistent.)

Brushing her hair herself meant she basically did nothing and was dropped off at school looking like she had just woken up for the day. When pickup time came, my wife would be mortified, so I called and gave her advanced notice. But when my wife got there for the afternoon pickup, our daughter's hair was brushed nicely, thanks to the kind intervention of her teacher. My wife thanked her and explained that she was not home that morning, so her dad [me] had to attempt the hair. The teacher responded with a snarky, "I figured." Should I be offended?

Desiring independence is a marker that a child is growing up, but it does not always mean the child is mature. Similarly, for the Christian, stubborn independence is a sign of immaturity. Even my daughter, who was showing independence in a developmentally appropriate way, was wrong about her skills and eventually had to have help. As Christians, we must never demand autonomy; the Christian life was never meant to be an independent life. We depend on the Lord first and foremost, and we also depend on one another. John Stott wrote that "one of our chief evangelical blind spots has been to overlook the central importance of the church. We tend to proclaim individual salvation without moving on to the saved community."[1]

At our local church, one of our core values is being "in community, not alone."[2] When a Christian neglects or rejects the local church and does not remain connected to the body of Christ, the Christian life distorts into something it was never designed to be: a solo endeavor. We are not sufficient on our own to serve God as he commanded the Christian life to be lived. I also do not understand why someone would want to live the Christian life alone, even if it was permissible. The local church is the story of people who are not figuratively able to get through life fixing their own hair. And it is also made up of those who can see and intervene with a bow in hand. Community is necessary. It is also theological. Not only are individuals made new in Jesus Christ, but we were also made a new (collective) people. Our faith is a corporate one, and God has not left us to be confused as to the outplaying of that reality. He has given us the church. As Jared C. Wilson puts it: "Our faith may be personal, but it's not meant to be private."[3]

Community is necessary.

Professing Christians must not merely attend a church service, but commit to a church body of believers. The best way for this to become a reality is through church membership, which allows our mindset to shift from "I go to this church" to "I belong to this church." I am in community as part of this family, not alone. In his article, "Young People, Church Membership Isn't Optional," Wilson continues that all Christians should commit to a local church because this is "how God has designed Christian growth to take place. We are individually members of a body" (Rom. 12:5; 1 Cor. 12:27) and "the community of believers is the ecosystem prescribed by God for healthy maturing in the faith."[4] We depend on one another to present ourselves mature in Christ, living as his people in a world that is not our home.

My great-grandfather was a proud Italian American. He was patriotic and loved being an American, but was extremely proud of and committed to his Italian roots. America was where he lived, but it was not where he was from. While he lived and worked in American culture, an important and meaningful aspect of his life was the local Italian club. It was a gathering place in Pittsburgh where he and others with Italian citizenship came together weekly to eat Italian food, speak their native language, enjoy fellowship with others from their same country, and enjoy their shared history together. I can imagine that this was an encouraging time each week for those who gathered. Residing in a foreign land is not easy.

Similarly, those who have placed their faith in Jesus Christ are not citizens of this world (Phil. 3:20). What a gift it is to gather weekly with our people and be reminded, as Paul charged the Philippians, to "stand firm in the Lord" (Phil. 4:1). Peter likewise wrote to the church, urging them "as strangers and exiles to abstain from sinful desires that wage war against the soul" (1 Pet. 2:11). The people of God are not of this world; we are citizens of heaven but exiles here. The temptations and pressure to conform to the worldviews, lifestyles, and idols of this world are ever present, and the weekly rhythm of coming together with other spiritual exiles and citizens of heaven is essential. We need to be around people who speak our language in a place where we can drink living water, feast from the Bread of Life, and be reminded of where we belong and especially to whom we belong.

Church membership identifies us with a specific spiritual family where we carry out the Bible's commands to live our Christian lives with one another. In fact, the Christian life is the story of "one anothers." These "one another" commands given throughout the Bible (and especially in the New Testament epistles) seem exhaustive and can feel overwhelming to the person trying to follow the Scriptures faithfully. But, like all of God's commands, they are for our good, and he gives us the power to carry them out. In his study guide, *Gospel in Life: Grace Changes Everything*, Tim Keller helpfully categorizes the "one another" commands into three buckets, which I will borrow here: affirm, share, and serve.[5] These categories give us a framework for how we should interact with one another.

INTERACTING WITH ONE ANOTHER

Affirm

Paul wrote to the church in Rome to "welcome one another, just as Christ also welcomed you, to the glory of

God" (Rom. 15:7). What Christ has done for us in showing us his kindness and grace, the church is to make visible by extending kindness and grace to one another. In a world of so much rejection, cynicism, resentment, and bitterness, the church should be an encouraging place for those trying to follow Jesus as they gather and fellowship with one another.

The church is also the context where believers affirm others' gifts and abilities to be used for ministry (Rom. 12:3–8). We can all tend to see ourselves as gifted in particular areas (and perhaps even neglect other areas out of fear of inadequacy), but if trusted fellow believers affirm our giftings, we should take that seriously. And, conversely, if they do not affirm something we think we are gifted in, we should take that seriously as well! Church members should have "concern for each other" (1 Cor. 12:25), a love that overflows for one another (1 Thess. 3:12), and should be kind and compassionate to one another (Eph. 4:32). What a gift to be a member of a local church! I am called to be and provide those things for others and can receive those gifts of encouragement to support my own journey of following Christ faithfully.

Share

My wife and I enjoy going out to dinner with friends and have often witnessed other couples opting to split their meal.

Every time I die a thousand deaths inside. When it comes to sharing my food, I'm like a toddler with toys. I understand sharing a meal can save money and keep one's personal figure intact, but I am not sitting at this great restaurant and giving somebody half of my steak. I did not promise my wife half of my filet when we exchanged wedding vows. However, that is because I am looking at sharing my food as a loss.

But the kind of sharing we are called to in Scripture is a gain, even when it requires sacrifice. We are called to something joyful: sharing our lives with one another. Christians are called to "be hospitable to one another" (1 Pet. 4:9), to encourage one another (Heb. 3:13; 1 Thess. 5:11), and as we share our lives together, to "carry one another's burdens" (Gal. 6:2).

The avenue through which we practice these commands is in the local church. It is impossible to carry this out as an occasional spectator who sits in a chair for an hour, hears a sermon, and leaves. Joining one's life to a local church is to invite oneself and others to Christian community. There God has beautifully designed the practice of loving one another to take place. Moving from a mindset of going to church to belonging to a church ignites the "one anothers" as we share our lives together.

As the early church was forming, Luke recorded that "all the believers were together and held all things in common" (Acts 2:44). We can safely assume that by having all things in common he did not mean they all had the same hobbies, food preferences, pet peeves, and favorite Old Testament prophet. What they had in common was a shared belief in the resurrected Christ and being part of God's mission to proclaim the good news of salvation and make disciples. The idea of "one anothers" is the active working of the grace of God bringing together believers from different backgrounds and stories by giving them the ultimate commonality: a life-changing belief in salvation alone through faith in the crucified and risen Messiah. As a result of what we believe to be true about Jesus, we share our lives with one another.

God uses the "one anothers" of the church for the strengthening of the body of Christ and the flourishing of the Christian community, and also for the sake of the lost world. The church members are to "live in harmony with one another" (Rom. 12:16) and agree with one another (1 Cor. 1:10). This is not uniformity, but rather a shared unity around their belief in the gospel and commitment to follow Jesus Christ. When the church lives in harmony and agreement, it can be a visual testimony in a world that rarely sees such a thing in our divisive and polarized society. In 1 Corinthians 6, Paul is concerned about lawsuits that existed among believers in the church. Paul is writing this letter because he is outraged that brother goes to court against brother and that it is before unbelievers (1 Cor. 6:6). The disputes within the family of

God were being displayed before unbelievers in the court. This is different from sharing hospitality with one another, and as a result, it has missional implications that can show unbelievers the church is no different in how they treat one another from the world. We share our lives together for the sake of the mission.

When the church lives in harmony and agreement, it can be a visual testimony in a world that rarely sees such a thing in our divisive and polarized society.

As the church practices the "one anothers," the world gets to see a visible portrait of the invisible reality of Christ's love for his people. The local church members love one another because Christ first loved them (1 John 4:10). Richard Lints defines the unity of the church as "the union of the people of God, in all their various distinctives and expressions, bound to God and to one another by the gospel."[6] We support one another by sharing our lives, in our church communities, "so that we can be coworkers with the truth" (3 John 8).

Serve

The last aspect of the "one anothers" Keller points to is the responsibility of the local church to serve. One way church members can serve one another is through mutual accountability. As the church members "provoke love and good works" (Heb. 10:24) in one another, they "pray for one another" (James 5:16) and "speak the truth" of the Scriptures (Eph. 4:25) to one another. In a society where defensiveness is a first instinct when confronted or corrected, church members can provide an environment where "all humility and gentleness, with patience, bearing with one another in love" (Eph. 4:2) is normal. There is no other institution in society where that is a reality. The local church is the best thing going.

Since Christ has served us in giving us his life, we serve one another. It completely goes against human nature to serve the interests of one another rather than our own. The thought of pleasing one another rather than prioritizing the self (Rom. 15:1–2) could be considered blasphemy by the standards of this world. But the church stands as a countercultural institution, focusing on Christ. The thought of serving one another sounds like a chore unless it is true that Christ first served us. The local church consists of people who have been served immeasurably by the work of Jesus Christ and now respond to the good news of the gospel by serving one another.

The church stands as a countercultural
institution, focusing on Christ.

CONCLUSION

Followers of Christ do not need to go on a scavenger hunt to find a place to live out the callings of affirming, sharing with, and serving the body of Christ. God has provided the means for us to carry out his calling and will for his people, and that is by being members of the church locally. Just as my daughter's teacher knew something was off when she saw Little Miss Bedhead, being known and in community gives us other sets of eyes who can spot when things are "off." And when a Christian is detached from a local church, something is certainly off. Let us be a people who do not aimlessly live our own idea of Christianity, but rather flourish in the abundant life of following Christ by joining his mission and the family he has redeemed.

Right before his arrest and impending crucifixion, Jesus prayed a powerful prayer for his disciples, recorded in John 17. He specifically prayed that in him their joy would be "complete" (v. 13). Jesus's prayer continues: "The world hated them because they are not of the world, just as I am not of the world. I am not praying that you take them out of the world but that you protect them from the evil one. They are not of the world, just as I am not of the world" (vv. 14–16). He goes on to pray for all of us who would believe in him through the disciples' message and that everyone in Christ would "all be one" (v. 21).

We are beneficiaries of that prayer, and we can see that the pattern for unity throughout the New Testament is churches being formed. The Christian life happens in community, not alone, under godly church leadership with a responsibility to guide the church to live faithfully. The local church, by God's help, can be the realization of the prayer of Christ for his followers.

DISCUSS AND REFLECT

1. In what ways is church something we are and something we do? Why is the both/and aspect important to understand?

2. What does the mindset of "beloning" to a church bring to the Christian life?

3. How do the "one anothers" shape the body of Christ into maturity?

4. Who are the "one anothers" that you can grow in practicing?

CHAPTER 3

Why Do We Preach the Bible?

AFTER OUR EASTER SERVICE several years ago, my family attended a lunch gathering with a few other families from our church. As I waited in line to pile ham on my plate, I said hello to one of the younger kids who was standing in front of me. She was around kindergarten age. I asked her how she liked the Easter service. I had changed clothes after the service and knew she did not recognize me as the pastor who had preached a couple of hours before. She answered, "It was okay."

"Just okay?" I asked, in what I am sure was an annoying dad-type tone.

"Yeah," she said, "the music was nice, but then this guy just went up there and talked for a long time. I'm not sure why he did that."

Well, the Scriptures tell us that God gives grace to the humble, so let's just say I had a lot of grace given to me in that moment, as the six-year-old was not impressed with my Easter sermon! Or, as she called it, my "long talk." If we put ourselves in her shoes for a moment, the question of why I went up there and talked for a while makes sense to ask. Why is preaching a sermon part of the church service?

The local church is the primary place of discipleship in the life of the believer, and nothing is more important in cultivating that than preaching the Bible. God's Word as the primary director of God's people is prominent throughout the storyline of the Bible. There are many ways we communicate with one another today (and the means increase faster than we can keep up), but the way God has communicated to his people has remained the same. It is through his Word, the Scriptures. In an ever-changing world, God's communication to his people has remained steadfast, authoritative, and relevant. "Faith comes from what is heard," the book of Romans tells us (10:17), and God is most certainly heard through the Scriptures.

> The local church is the primary place of discipleship in the life of the believer, and nothing is more important in cultivating that than preaching the Bible.

I remember taking a hearing exam as a child as part of a health screening at my elementary school. Wearing headphones, I was told to raise my hand each time I heard a beep. I was so scared to miss one of the beeps that I raised my hand whenever I heard something I thought was a beep. My hand may have been raised the entire time. Perhaps I have hearing issues that never got addressed! It can be similarly paralyzing when we think we must listen for God's voice. Thankfully, God has not left us to worry about whether that was a "beep" from him in our figurative headphones of life. God has given us the Scriptures. A cacophony of competing noises clamors for our attention today, but when we turn to the Bible, we need not feel confusion over what is God's Word and what is a separate noise masking as God's voice. God speaks through his Word.

Regular Bible reading is an important aspect of the life of the individual Christian, but another critical component is to hear the Scriptures read aloud and have them taught and preached to us. In his book about preaching, Jonathan Griffiths notes that preaching in the New Testament is a public declaration of God's Word which stands in line with Old Testament prophetic ministry.[1] It is an intentional forthtelling of God's Word. God has spoken and continues to speak whenever his Word is read and declared. Isaiah 55:10–11 tells us that God says of his own Word:

"For just as rain and snow fall from heaven
and do not return there
without saturating the earth
and making it germinate and sprout,
and providing seed to sow
and food to eat,
so my word that comes from my mouth
will not return to me empty,
but it will accomplish what I please
and will prosper in what I send it to do."

Through the reading and preaching and hearing of God's Word, God changes those who hear it. God's Word can accomplish things that nothing else can, and in it we find everything we need for "life and godliness" (2 Pet. 1:3). Timothy George wrote: "The Word of God was meant not only to be read, studied, translated, memorized, and meditated on. It was also to be embodied in the life and worship of the church."[2] Throughout Scripture, we see that the declaration of God's words to his people is what calls them to repentance and strengthens their faith. Since this is the scriptural pattern, the church is right to place the preaching of God's Word as the centerpiece of the gathering of God's people. George adds that "the sermon is a vital and integral part of corporate worship."[3]

The chief focus of preaching is to display the grand story of the Bible, ultimately understood in the life, death, and resurrection of Jesus Christ. Scripture tells us that in these last days, "he has spoken to us by his Son" (Heb. 1:2). Preaching exalts the name of Jesus Christ from the Scriptures, of which he is the main theme. The Messiah and Redeemer the Old Testament promised and awaited has been fully provided in Jesus Christ.

BUILDING UP THE BODY THROUGH PREACHING

The primary objective that preaching should accomplish in a church setting is twofold. The first is the building up of the body through the primary means God has given to grow us as disciples: his Word. Church members, "like newborn infants, desire the pure milk of the word, so that by it you may grow up into your salvation" (1 Pet. 2:2).

Good preaching nourishes.

Peter pointed to the Scriptures as the nourishment for the church. When my children were newborns, nothing triggered a loud cry like me having to adjust the bottle for just a moment to reposition myself while holding them. Anytime

I briefly pulled the bottle out of their mouths, they lost their minds. But as soon as I popped the bottle back in their mouths, there was peace.

As infants, all four of my children desired milk. It was their livelihood. My wife joked that during her first few months with each of our children, she felt like her primary purpose in life was keeping them alive. There is much truth to that statement, as any nursing mom of a newborn can attest, I am certain. The means of their survival was the milk their mother provided. Milk is not only how babies grow, but also how they continue to live. Without the proper nutrients they cannot survive. Peter writes that Christians should see the Scriptures in that manner and, as a result, desire to receive them. A church that does not have the preaching of the Word of God as a priority will be a malnourished, unhealthy body of believers.

Paul instructed Timothy, a young pastor he was mentoring, to "preach the word; be ready in season and out of season; correct, rebuke, and encourage with great patience and teaching" (2 Tim. 4:2). This was the charge: preach the Word of God to the people of God. In every season. When the first Christians started gathering together following the ascension of the resurrected Jesus Christ, "they devoted themselves to the apostles' teaching" (Acts 2:42). Here the church has not even begun organizing, but the teachings were already central in their gatherings together. They knew they needed the Word of God to survive.

Good preaching corrects.

Errors of misunderstanding concerning Scripture can be corrected through preaching, whereas false teachers lead the church away from the truth of the Scriptures. False teachings usually add additional requirements to the Scriptures, altering the gospel, or they take away from the Bible's words, commands, and truths to cover up for biblical content that people simply do not like. As the church, we need to see preaching as an act of grace that God offers his people to keep us from being led astray.

Good preaching rebukes when necessary.

If there are sins in our life that we must repent, the Scriptures will make that a reality. We need preaching in our lives from our church to point us away from the lusts of this world and to enjoy our life with God. Since we believe the promises of God, we can receive rebuke humbly, seeing it as an act of grace, knowing the rebuke does not change our standing with God in terms of our salvation and that God is using the preaching of his Word to keep us from a life that resembles what he has saved us from. As a shepherd uses his staff to redirect his sheep from harm, God uses correction and rebuke in preaching to save us from spiritual danger.

As a shepherd uses his staff to redirect his sheep from harm, God uses correction and rebuke in preaching to save us from spiritual danger.

Good preaching encourages.

Living in a world that is not our home can be a place of tremendous discouragement for the church. The gospel is mocked, Christian teachings are ridiculed, and the presence of brokenness is all around. Preaching encourages the church from the Scriptures to press on and remain faithful because God is faithful. The means of encouragement for the church is to hear again the promises of God, from the Word of God, remembered and treasured in community, together. "God is for us" (Rom. 8:31), and nothing can ever separate us from his love (vv. 38–39).

PRESENTING THE GOSPEL THROUGH PREACHING

The second important aspect of why a church preaches the Bible every Sunday is to assure that people in the room who are not believers clearly hear the gospel of Jesus Christ. Mature church members should expect and even demand that unbelievers attending their church never leave the parking lot without hearing the truth of the gospel of Jesus Christ during the sermon. In fact, that is why we invite friends to come. Yes, you may have already shared the good news with them, but you also desire for it to be declared and explained in the context of the church through preaching. The sermon's content does not need to be minimized to accommodate an unbeliever, but the preaching should be clear.

It is also helpful for church members to be reminded weekly of what some might view as elementary truths. As the pastor explains the gospel to attending unbelievers, the church is being edified by being reminded of the amazing truth that they are "saved by grace through faith" (Eph. 2:8). In a world where we are constantly tempted to rely on our own effort, we must regularly be pointed back to grace. Matt Morton from Dallas Theological Seminary wrote that "even though we heard the good news of Jesus last Sunday, we need to hear it again this Sunday. Good preachers pretty much say the same things over and over again, in fact, because they know how desperately we need reminding."[4]

I get asked by young aspiring pastors if I primarily speak to the unbeliever or the believer on Sunday mornings. I believe the task of the preacher is to edify the church. I preach to church members, but I always have guests in mind. The Bible is for both. If the unbeliever is going to understand his need for salvation found only in Christ, it is going to be because God allows him to open his eyes to see the Scriptures. Apart from the Spirit of God, the Bible is folly to any unbeliever. As I lift the name of Jesus and preach the Bible, I am declaring these truths to the church while being mindful of the need to be clear in explanation to all. I am convinced that mature Christians are those who desire for everyone to understand in a local church preaching setting.

And, for those who are not doing the preaching, we should prepare our hearts to hear and receive the Word of God. Distractions are everywhere, and preoccupation can be a big struggle for many. There is always something else to think about, an errand to run after the church service is over, and a child to transport across town for the activity of the day. When the pastor steps into the pulpit and opens the Scriptures, know that in hearing the sermon, you are experiencing God's Word as God intended it to be heard, through the medium of preaching. As you pray for focus, pray also for your heart not to be hardened by sin and for God to prepare it to receive his Word. It is also important to be sensitive to how the Lord wants you to respond based on what you have heard from his Word. Do you need to repent from a sin to forgive a person or promise to hold onto someone tightly? Hearing the Word through preaching often calls for a response in our heart, mind, and life.

CONCLUSION

I still look back and chuckle at the young girl whose take-away from the Easter service was that some guy went up there and talked for a longtime. Maybe I needed to sharpen my preaching skills to keep her attention. But the good news for all of us is that even if the messenger needs some work in his delivery, the presence of preaching need not change. It should be the central aspect of the church gathering, where faith is strengthened by what is heard, and the promise is believed that God will not allow his Word to return empty (Isa. 55:11). When the Word is being faithfully preached, something significant is always happening.

DISCUSS AND REFLECT

1. Why does preaching matter?

2. Is preaching the most important thing in a church gathering? Why or why not?

3. Why does the believer need the preaching of the gospel when he/she already knows and believes the gospel?

4. "When the word of God is being preached, there is always something significant happening." Do you believe this is true? If so, how can we know this, and what is actually happening?

CHAPTER 4

Why Do We Gather Every Week?

THE FIRST DAY OF school has become quite the spectacle in our society. If you don't believe me, just scroll through social media in August. There's a nervous feeling of anticipation, kids lay out their clothes the night before, and brand-new school supplies are packed in brand-new backpacks. After a summer of staying up late watching movies, swimming until dark in the neighborhood pool, and taking trips out of town as a family, the night before the first day of school resets everything back to normal. Proper bedtimes are restored, and parents run through mental checklists, making sure everything is set for the big day. After an earlier wake-up time than what was practiced all summer, a first-day-of-school breakfast is served, pictures are taken in first-day-of-school outfits, and off the kids go to the start of a new school year.

While I am not going to be "that guy" and suggest we approach every Saturday night before church with the same kind of excitement and anticipation, I do think there is a lesson to learn about how we view the coming morning when it is significant to us. We prepare and plan accordingly. The night before the first day of school is different from any other night of the summer because kids have somewhere important to be. Christian families should see Sunday morning as such a normal part of life that when we go to sleep the night before, it should be with anticipation and preparation. It is not the time to forget to set an alarm or have a lazy summer morning like a middle-school student on school break. We have somewhere to be, and that is with our church family.

It has been commonly said that the local church is the hope of the world. This points to God's plan and design for his people to worship him, make disciples, and evangelize the lost world. But where do we get the notion of gathering weekly? Whose idea was it?

As John Piper lays out helpfully in one of his "Ask Pastor John" episodes,[1] Christianity has its roots in Judaism. And a weekly worship gathering was baked into the identity of Jewish culture because it was commanded by God. Every seventh day on the weekly calendar, the Jewish people gathered and worshipped God. That seventh day was called the Sabbath, a weekly rhythm instituted by God for rest and worship. It even has its place in the Ten Commandments, in which the Jewish people were instructed to "remember the Sabbath day" and "keep it holy" (Exod. 20:8).

Piper points out that we can know Jews were still doing this in the first century when the early Christian church was forming because, in the book of Acts, Paul would enter the synagogue on the Sabbath and proclaim the name of Jesus Christ. He entered there on the last day of the week because the people he wanted to evangelize would already be gathered there, as was their duty, custom, and tradition as God's people. This Saturday gathering was in every sense a regular rhythm of life as worshippers of God.

Eventually, the practice for those who believed that Jesus Christ was the Messiah would change the gathering of believers to Sunday, which would become known as the Lord's Day, due to the resurrection of Christ happening on the first day of the week, not the last (the Sabbath). This shift occurred fairly early, since we are told specifically that the Christians gathered "on the first day of the week" (Acts 20:7). Now, the risen Messiah, rather than Jewish heritage and tradition, is the source of identity for Christians, but a regular rhythm of gathering to worship God is something he ordained since he first called a people to himself.

If one grew up in a Jewish home in the first century, going to a worship gathering at the synagogue would be the regular Sabbath-day activity. It was foundational to their cultural identity and their faith in the one true God who led their ancestors out of Egypt. The Sabbath worship was as normal as eating and sleeping. During the weekly worship, they would be reminded about the great things God had done for his people and recite prayers together, giving thanks to God in worship for his faithfulness to them for generations.

When it comes to modern-day Christians and the Lord's Day, it is easy to slip out of the routine of the weekly gathering that has been a critical regularity in the lives of believers for centuries. But it should not be so! I remind the local church I pastor that Sunday-morning church is a Saturday-night decision. As evening approaches on Saturday, it is important for Christians to keep Sunday morning in mind, knowing that when they wake up, they will be getting ready to gather with their local church. That is what followers of Jesus Christ do on Sundays. Like the Jews before us, we need the weekly reminder of God's faithfulness and the corporate declaration of our allegiance to him.

Ironically, the same generation of parents who get overly hyped for their kids' first days of school are often disinterested in attending their own school reunions. Perhaps because of social media and our constant awareness of everyone's whereabouts, high school reunions have lost their luster in our culture. As someone who has attended and loved my high school reunions so far, it is strange to me that something that only happens once a decade fails to generate enthusiasm, excitement, and participation.

If something that happens so infrequently brings such a feeling of indifference, it is easy to think that something scheduled weekly, such as a church gathering, will be seen as anticlimactic and okay to miss. That is why our understanding of the *why* is so important. John Piper said that God's Word "calls us to regular, weekly expressions of our corporate joy and thankfulness before God in worship—not just isolated Christian individuals scattered around but corporate gatherings praying and singing and hearing God's word and celebrating the ordinances of Jesus."[2]

WHY WE GATHER

We gather every week because God's Word calls us to this as his people.

That reason should be enough for us. He has prescribed it, and the early Christians in the Scriptures practiced and modeled this calling from God. One could claim we go to church weekly because we are Christians, and that would be sufficient. It shows spiritual maturity when we gather with our church even when we do not feel like it. In fact, you could even say that the most important times to be at church are when we do not want to be there. Then we are reminded that God's faithfulness never wavers, and that to be a part of his family is an act of grace he has richly blessed us with in Christ.

We gather weekly because we are (or should be) a thankful people.

We come together to give praise to God, the one who took us from spiritual death to spiritual life. Being reminded of his works should produce joy; corporately expressing that together enriches our souls.

We go to church weekly because we need it in our lives.

For the individual follower of Christ, worship is a moment-by-moment recognition of and response to the goodness and grace of God in our lives, but it is also an intentional, corporate action as prescribed by God. Christians live in a world that is not our home every other hour of the day and week; we need to gather with the citizens of heaven. Six days in between sounds like a long time, and we should see the first day of the week as a means of survival and fuel to flourish as the salt and light which Jesus called us to be.

WHAT WE ACCOMPLISH

So we have some whys. But there are also important aspects of what the weekly gathering accomplishes and points us toward.

The gathered church forshadows heaven.

In chapters 4–5 of the book of Revelation, we get a glimpse of how the local church gathering foreshadows what is experienced in heaven. The corporate worship gathers us around God's throne and centers the church on his grace.[3] Revelation 4:9–11 reads:

> Whenever the living creatures give glory, honor, and thanks to the one seated on the throne, the one who lives forever and ever, the twenty-four elders fall down before the one seated on the throne and worship the one who lives forever and ever. They cast their crowns before the throne and say,
>
> > Our Lord and God,
> > you are worthy to receive
> > glory and honor and power,
> > because you have created all things,
> > and by your will
> > they exist and were created.

The gathered church gets a taste of the throne room of heaven as God's people around the world worship the one true God who is on the throne. In the Lord's Prayer, Jesus teaches us to pray "on earth as it is in heaven" (Matt. 6:10). Reading that glimpse into heaven in Revelation, I can say that the local church gathered is the closest picture of that reality until he returns.

By worshipping the one who is on the throne, we are likewise proclaiming in action that we are not on the throne. Corporate worship pushes back against the self-exalting posture and values of the world around us. Russian pastor Yuri Sipko instructed believers to "confess him and worship him in such a way that people can see this world is a lie."[4] As we gather, we push back against the world in worship by proclaiming Jesus is Lord and that we are not.

Jesus claimed the church is "the light of the world. A city situated on a hill cannot be hidden. No one lights a lamp and puts it under a basket, but rather on a lampstand, and it gives light for all who are in the house" (Matt. 5:14–15). The church shines the light into the world, as the gathered church is the earthly portrait of the forever reality of Christ's kingdom and reign.

The church shines the light into the world, as the gathered church is the earthly portrait of the forever reality of Christ's kingdom and reign.

The gathered church also points us to the gospel story.

In Revelation 5, notice it is not one individual person having his personal time of worship, but rather, gathered around the throne, the angels and elders (holding the prayers of the believers) through song proclaimed:

> You are worthy to take the scroll
> and to open its seals,
> because you were slaughtered,
> and you purchased people
> for God by your blood
> from every tribe and language
> and people and nation. (v. 9)

We proclaim as churches now what will be proclaimed for eternity by the saints in heaven—that Jesus is the one who sits in on the throne and has accomplished redemption and salvation for his people. The apostle John wrote:

> I heard every creature in heaven, on earth, under the earth, on the sea, and everything in them say,
>
> > Blessing and honor and glory and power
> > be to the one seated on the throne,
> > and to the Lamb, forever and ever! (v. 13)

CONCLUSION

We make a Saturday-night decision to attend Sunday church because, there, we get a foretaste of heaven and participate in the worship of the one forever on the throne. What a privilege to worship the one true King, together as those who are not of this world. Jesus Christ has ushered in a new kingdom, and while the worship of Christ is every moment for the church, the members of the body come together weekly to participate together in corporate worship of the one who died for them, has risen, and will come again to make all things new.

DISCUSS AND REFLECT

1. Why has the weekend gathering of the church lost some of its luster among Christians?

2. Sunday morning church being a Saturday night decision means that attending church has become a spiritual discipline in our age. How can you make going to church a regular rhythm in your life, and how can you encourage other believers to make this a healthy habit?

3. Why do you believe Christians need the weekly worship service in their lives?

CHAPTER 5

Why Do We Sing?

I PLANNED A TRIP to a big city with my oldest son to attend a Major League Baseball game for his birthday. When I went online to book a hotel, the regular chain hotels in the city were between triple and quadruple what seemed like the normal rate. I then looked at the surrounding suburbs to see if several miles out of town there was a reasonable hotel rate we could find. Same story. Nothing. I made a joke to my wife that Taylor Swift must be performing in the city that weekend. My wife searched her tour online, and sure enough, my random side comment was the reality. Taylor Swift was playing at the National Football League stadium in the middle of downtown. The hotel rates now had an explanation. We wound up staying in a different state. Seriously.

A major pop concert with the star power of Taylor Swift is a phenomenon in our society. Her concerts sell out football stadiums, and everyone sings at the top of their lungs. The singing from the crowd is often so loud it drowns out the instruments in the band. A performer can simply point to a section of the arena, and everyone will shout. The way people respond at a concert is something to behold. Those in the crowd who bought a ticket know every word of every song and serve as participants from their seats. This is different from a jazz concert or a symphony where the audience sits back and enjoys the music.

While a church gathering should never be a pop concert, it was also never designed to be a jazz performance with detached audience members watching quietly. Somehow, nobody considers it strange or awkward when people sing loudly at a concert, locked into every word from their favorite musical artist, yet at a church gathering, that part of worship can be an adjustment for some. The result is onlooking and listening rather than participating.

Why is singing along with Taylor Swift about her ex-boyfriends normal, but singing at church is strange? It is perhaps because people have not been instructed that singing is something the people of God do when they come together. Throughout the Scriptures, God's people sing in response to his goodness and greatness in what can be considered a musical form of prayer and praise. Singing can also serve as a type of instruction of the truth of God's Word and encouragement among a congregation. Paul told the Ephesian church to speak "to one another in psalms, hymns, and spiritual songs, singing and making music with your heart to the Lord" (Eph. 5:19). Singing to the Lord is a historical activity of the people of God.

WHY WE SING

Singing is commanded.

Psalm 100 in its entirety says:

> Let the whole earth shout triumphantly to the Lord!
> Serve the Lord with gladness;
> come before him with joyful songs.
> Acknowledge that the Lord is God.
> He made us, and we are his—
> his people, the sheep of his pasture.
> Enter his gates with thanksgiving
> and his courts with praise.
> Give thanks to him and bless his name.
> For the Lord is good, and his faithful love endures forever;
> his faithfulness, through all generations.

The psalmist calls the people of God to praise him in thanksgiving for his faithfulness to them. In doing so, they come before God singing joyful songs. This psalm comes in sequence after a group of psalms declaring the greatness of God. The climax is the response of Psalm 100: singing to the Lord for who he is and what he has done. Notice the use of words like *triumphantly* and *gladness* and *joyful* in those first few verses of Psalm 100. This indicates what sort of posture we should have. James Montgomery Boice said that "the people of God are to praise God loudly because they are happy with Him."[1] What a great reminder. If our musical worship feels cold or lifeless, what does that say about our affection toward God?

Martin Luther claimed that music should be praised "as second only to the Word of God. That is why there are so many psalms and songs. This precious gift has been bestowed upon men alone, to remind them that they are created to praise and magnify the Lord."[2]

Luther also added: "Any who remain unaffected [by music] are clodhoppers indeed and are fit to hear only the words of dung-poets and the music of pigs."[3] I think what Luther would be saying if speaking to a twenty-first-century audience is that singing songs to the Lord does something in our hearts, or it should. It certainly gives us reminders of the Lord's faithfulness to his people. The songs of the Old

Testament, sung by the Hebrew people, are often reflections on the different times and ways God had delivered them or their ancestors. For example, Exodus 15 tells us of a song Moses and Miriam led with the Israelites immediately following God's miraculous provision at the Red Sea. Psalm 105 is a long recap of Israel's history and God's faithful hand on them to that point.

Singing helps us remember.

Music has a way of taking us back to an era. I lived my teenage years in the 1990s, and to this day, listening to the "90s on 9" station on my satellite radio is something I enjoy because it reminds me of happy times and memories of coming of age with the friends of my youth. Certain songs remind me of being at the beach or driving back after a football game. Reflecting can produce joy, and music has a unique way of transporting us back into a memory. I know many songs from the 1950s because I rode in the back seat as a little kid as my dad played songs from his era on oldies radio. I do not want to think about the fact that my teenaged music of the 1990s is as far removed from today as my dad's "oldies" music was when I was a kid! But that music was comforting to him the same way my music is comforting to me.

As people who live by faith in the promises of God, people living between the times of Christ's ascension and his second coming, we need regular reminders to take us back to how God has kept every promise to his people and that he will return to wipe away every tear and make all things new. Second to hearing the preaching of Scripture, congregational singing (together as a church family) takes us back to the source, the goodness and grace of our God. Congregational singing is a crucial element of a local church gathering as "the word of Christ dwell[s] richly among [us], in all wisdom teaching and admonishing one another through psalms, hymns, and spiritual songs, singing to God with gratitude in [our] hearts" (Col. 3:16).

Singing brings comfort.

Singing together also serves to comfort the church in times of sorrow, doubt, and pain. The familiar hymn "Great Is Thy Faithfulness" is an example of how singing can point us to important reminders of God's goodness amid hardship. The song, written by Thomas Chisholm, references Lamentations 3:22–23, in which Jeremiah is lamenting the state of God's people in their sin. The Old Testament prophet begins in anguish, writing:

How she sits alone,
the city once crowded with people!
She who was great among the nations
has become like a widow.
The princess among the provinces
has been put to forced labor.

She weeps bitterly during the night,
with tears on her cheeks.
There is no one to offer her comfort,
not one from all her lovers.
All her friends have betrayed her;
they have become her enemies. (Lam. 1:1–2)

By every measurable assumption, one would conclude that Jeremiah would not be in the mood to sing as he writes such painful words about what has become of the people of Israel. He describes the scene as one where "all her people groan" (v. 11). Jeremiah says, "I weep because of these things; my eyes flow with tears" (v. 16). Think of the person walking into a church gathering on a Sunday morning who has had a week of weeping or a season of experiencing brokenness and pain. This is Jeremiah looking upon Jerusalem: "my groans are many, and I am sick at heart" (v. 22). While the setting and circumstances are different, you may have people reluctantly walking into your church's service with intense burdens as the band begins the first song. Jeremiah laments, "My future is lost, as well as my hope from the LORD" (3:18). Then the state of Jeremiah's demeanor and mindset suddenly changes because he remembers:

> Yet I call this to mind,
> and therefore I have hope:
>
> Because of the LORD's faithful love
> we do not perish,
> for his mercies never end.
> They are new every morning;
> great is your faithfulness! (vv. 21–23)

The person walking in the door on Sunday morning hearing the congregation sing "Great Is Thy Faithfulness" can have a Jeremiah moment of remembering that while the circumstances of the world may feel like too much to bear, God remains faithful to his people and his word; he will never abandon or forsake us. Remembering God's faithfulness caused Jeremiah to write:

> For the Lord
> will not reject us forever.
> Even if he causes suffering,
> he will show compassion
> according to the abundance of his faithful love.
> (Lam. 3:31–32)

When the singing of the congregation continues to point people in praise to the goodness of God, it provides reminders through the emotion-stirring medium of music that God can be trusted, this world is temporary, and God's promises are eternal. He is faithful, indeed. It is important to hear that through preaching, but it is also part of God's plan for his people to proclaim his faithfulness from their own mouths, together, though singing praise to him.

Singing helps us belong.

Congregational singing unites the church. We sing together under the shared belief as church members that Jesus Christ is Lord. People from different backgrounds come together at a Taylor Swift concert and during that time are in unison (and figurative harmony) with one another. During football games, fans unite in singing the team fight song after a touchdown. People stop whatever they are doing and remove their hats when the national anthem is played. People who followed the Grateful Dead band across the country to hear them play music were known as "Deadheads." Throughout distinct cultures and societies, songs unite.

If we can unite over a sports team or a pop star, how much greater a uniting force should the Creator of the universe be—the one who loved us so much that he gave his only Son to be the propitiation of our sins? How much more reason to unite around song than the truth that Jesus Christ has risen from the grave and currently is reigning and ruling for all eternity? Scripture tells us that creation itself declares the glory of God, that the skies sing it out! "Day after day they pour out speech; night after night they communicate knowledge" (Ps. 19:2). Jesus even told us that if we did not sing his praises, the rocks themselves would pick up the slack (Luke 19:40).

We sing together under the shared belief as church members that Jesus Christ is Lord.

Andrew Wilson wrote that "when we sing together as a church, we are not just aligning ourselves with each other, or with the created order as a whole. We are aligning it with the One who sings loud songs of exultation over his children, and who finished the Last Supper by singing a hymn with his friends."[4] What an amazing picture. Singing God's praises unites us with God's people, God's creation, and God himself.

Not only is our God kind to give us such a beautiful thing as music, but he has wired its potency into our brain chemistry. Research shows that singing together with others has numerous health benefits,[5] most likely because it heightens our sense of belonging. Jennie Pollock writes that, while "some suggest this is an 'evolved behavior,' . . . to the Christian it sounds more like a gift of God. . . . Singing together builds community, it strengthens our bonds with one another. And it can bring life to one another."[6] Pollock adds that not only does it matter that we sing, but it also matters what we sing. Music "forms us and shapes us around the truths we sing about our God, his salvation and his call on our lives. It embeds those truths in us and binds us to one another in a way that no other practice can."[7]

Singing can be learned.

Singing in church is a learned practice. For some, singing aloud seems foreign and uncomfortable. It might take some time and effort to learn the songs commonly sung at one's local church and embrace new songs being written and introduced to the congregation, and there is certainly more than one right way for churches to sing. If one visits seventeen different churches in seventeen different nations, they will likely find seventeen unique styles of music and congregational singing. The common factor will be that the churches sing songs. Some will be quiet, others loud. You will find singing accompanied by choirs, and others with someone standing behind a microphone playing a guitar. Some churches have no music accompaniment and sing a cappella; others have a powerful pipe organ or a rock-and-roll style band. The point is that different means and cultures and approaches are all used for the purpose of praising God through singing. Methods change, but the praise of the people should not. We will be singing for all eternity to the King of kings, and the primary place of practice the Lord has designed for us is the local church, united together in song to the one we believe is worthy of our praise.

> Sing a new song to the LORD;
> let the whole earth sing to the LORD.
> Sing to the LORD, bless his name;
> proclaim his salvation from day to day.
> (Ps. 96:1–2)

We will be singing for all eternity to the King of kings, and the primary place of practice the Lord has designed for us is the local church, united together in song to the one we believe is worthy of our praise.

This, as his people, is what we do together.

DISCUSS AND REFLECT

1. Why is singing at church weird for some people? Has it ever been strange to you?

2. What is the purpose of singing in church? How is it different than merely listening to someone sing a song?

3. Do you have a favorite hymn or church song? What makes it resonate with you?

4. How can you still sing to God when you don't feel like it at church?

5. Has singing in church ever brought you comfort? How so?

CHAPTER 6

Why Do We Take the Lord's Supper?

IN MOST CASES, AN individual either has a strong long-term memory or a strong short-term memory. (It would be helpful to be great at both.) One might hear someone say he can recite verbatim the dialogue of a scene from a movie from twenty years ago but cannot remember what he was supposed to pick up at the grocery store on the drive home from work. A strong long-term memory can garner admiration as you recall events, dates, and facts from years ago, and a poor short-term memory can get you into trouble. Have you ever forgotten to pick up your kids from school? A big whoops and short-term memory lapse. Yet somehow, you remember the names of the entire USA gold-medal-winning women's gymnastics team for the 1996 Olympics. (My wife can name all of them.)

In the Christian life, we have established that the local church is where we are designed to flourish in pursuit of Christ. And part of the role of the church gathered is to help the collective long-term memory, producing worship and faithfulness in the here and now by remembering what has been accomplished and what is promised. Long-term remembering fuels moment-by-moment living for Christ. We are to remember what God has done in the past and how that matters today.

A primary way the people of God have remembered God's faithfulness and work on their behalf has been through a meal. The Old Testament gives descriptions of many annual feasts and festivals the Israelites were to conduct in remembrance of particular events of God's goodness. One of the most prominent ones was the Passover meal, which commemorates what God did in establishing his people after leading them out of slavery in Egypt and from under Pharaoh's rule. The beginning chapters of Exodus walk us through the building tensions, culminating in a miraculous deliverance for God's people.

God called Moses (famously via a burning bush) to approach Pharaoh and request freedom for the enslaved Israelites. Not surprisingly, Pharaoh scoffed at the idea and refused. Despite many warnings and plagues issued to Egypt, the stubborn and hard-hearted leader refused to free the Hebrew people as God had commanded him repeatedly through the demands of Moses. After Egypt endured nine plagues, God gave a final warning about a plague that would bring judgment through the death of each firstborn son, by the coming of the angel of death in the middle of the night. But God gave specific instructions to his own people on how they could be spared this judgment. He provided salvation by instructing them to slaughter lambs and to put the blood from the slaughtered lamb on the doorframes of their residences. If the blood of the lamb was on their doorframe, the angel bringing judgment would pass over the homes. They would be spared God's judgment by the blood of the lamb. Their firstborn sons would be untouched because the death of the lamb served as a substitute.

Scripture tells us that all firstborn sons were lost in Egypt that night, except for those who had sheltered themselves under the blood. As a result of this devastation, Pharaoh not only freed the Israelites, but he feminine also pushed them out. They began their exodus out of Egypt to the land God would prepare for them. God instructed them to have a meal, the supper of lamb, with bitter herbs and unleavened bread, as an annual memorial of that fateful day. This would be known as the Passover meal (Exod. 12) and would be eaten annually by the Jewish people for generations. Practicing Jews still observe Passover today as they remember the night God brought deliverance to the people and passed over the homes covered by the blood of the lamb.

In the New Testament, Jesus introduced the ordinance of the Lord's Supper prior to his betrayal and arrest. *The New City Catechism* defines *ordinances* as "given by God and instituted by Christ, namely baptism and the Lord's Supper . . . visible signs and seals that we are bound together as a community of faith by his death and resurrection."[1]

Professor Gregg Allison, who has written extensively on the church, defines *ordinance* as "a Christian rite, associated with tangible elements (water; bread and wine), that is celebrated by the church of Jesus Christ. The term is closely associated with the word *sacrament*, which is an outward and visible sign of an inward and invisible grace."[2] Breaking from the Roman Catholic terminology of *sacrament*, the Protestant church uses the term *ordinance*, which Allison notes is to refer to these practices being "ordained, or instituted, by Christ Himself."[3] Protestant churches traditionally hold to two ordinances for the church: the Lord's Supper and baptism. Allison adds that one of three generally held positions on what the ordinances do is to "symbolize the faith and obedience of the people of God. . . . The ordinances are opportunities for their recipients to express their allegiance to Christ."[4]

While most Christians do not observe Jewish Passover, the new meal Jesus instituted during his Last Supper with his disciples has deep ties to the Passover meal. They were gathered to celebrate Passover. In fact, Jesus gave a new understanding to his disciples, tying it to the reality that he is the true Passover Lamb, who would shed his blood for the sins of the world. His death would be a substitutionary death in the place of all who would come to repent and believe. He would take on the judgment of sin as the sacrificial Lamb of God. What an amazing thing to think about! These followers gathered with their friend and rabbi to observe a familiar religious ceremony when he says, "This is all about me. This protection God has provided from wrath—it comes by my blood."

When Jesus first came onto the public scene in ministry, John the Baptist proclaimed: "Look, the Lamb of God!" (John 1:36). John was pointing to Jesus Christ as the true Passover Lamb. The blood of this Lamb would rescue and save from the just judgment of God over sin. Now, instead of remembering the symbolic slaughtered lambs of the Old Testament covenant, we commemorate the Lamb, slain for us. By taking this meal and remembering the true Passover Lamb, Christians are strengthened in their resolve to follow Christ and be united together with all those who are allegiant to him.

At the last Passover meal of Jesus's earthly life, now immortalized as the Last Supper, Jesus "took bread, gave thanks, broke it, gave it to them, and said, 'This is my body, which is given for you. Do this in remembrance of me.' In the same way he also took the cup after supper and said, 'This cup is the new covenant in my blood, which is poured out for you'" (Luke 22:19–20). Even though his crucifixion was just hours away, the disciples did not yet know what he was referring to or what was to come, but it would change the entire world. Similar in timing to the Passover instructions God gave to the Israelites before the exodus, Jesus was preparing his disciples the night before an earth-shattering moment. Jonathan Griffiths writes: "As the Passover meal served as a foundational meal of the old covenant, taking place on the brink of the foundational saving act of the covenant (the Exodus from Egypt), so the Lord's Supper was the foundational meal of the new covenant, taking place on the brink of the saving work that Jesus would achieve on the cross."[5]

Paul, later writing to the Corinthian church, recounts:

> For I received from the Lord what I also passed on to you: On the night when he was betrayed, the Lord Jesus took bread, and when he had given thanks, broke it, and said, "This is my body, which is for you. Do this in remembrance of me."
>
> In the same way also he took the cup, after supper, and said, "This cup is the new covenant in my blood. Do this, as often as you drink it, in remembrance of me." For

WHY DO WE TAKE THE LORD'S SUPPER?

as often as you eat this bread and drink the cup, you proclaim the Lord's death until he comes. (1 Cor. 11:23–26)

TAKING THE LORD'S SUPPER

We take the Lord's Supper in the local church because we "proclaim the Lord's death until he comes."

We remind ourselves of the gospel story until Jesus returns, just as he ordained us to do. It points us back to Christ, just as the children of Israel were pointed back to the Passover. Generations after their ancestors had been enslaved in Egypt, their hearts and minds would return there through the Passover meal to remember the faithfulness of God and to declare allegiance to him over the false and pagan gods. It is not random that once the church was established at Pentecost, those first Christians "devoted themselves . . . to the breaking of bread" (Acts 2:42). In the hostile world they were about to encounter, the gospel story would not be merely a reminder, but their lifeline. It would be their only hope.

The writer of Hebrews instructed the believers to keep their eyes on Jesus (Heb. 12:2). He is the one who endured the cross, and the regular focus on that truth would allow them not to lose hope (v. 3). When I take the Lord's Supper with my fellow church members in our Lord's Day gathering, it strengthens my faith and brings me joy as I think about God's people who went before us who observed the Passover. They remembered what God had done to deliver them and anticipated the fulfillment of the promise that a Redeemer would spiritually deliver God's people once and for all. That promise led the writer of Hebrews to point to those believers long before the coming of Christ, who "experienced mockings and scourgings, as well as bonds and imprisonment. They were stoned, they were sawed in two, they died by the sword, they wandered about in sheepskins, in goatskins, destitute, afflicted, and mistreated" (11:36–37). They kept the faith, even though they had not seen the fulfillment of the promise in their lifetimes. As I take the bread and the juice, often known as the "elements," I am reminded that all the promises of God have been answered "Yes" in Jesus Christ (2 Cor. 1:20). Just as they remembered and anticipated, we now rejoice in his coming, remembering his sacrifice and anticipating his return.

FENCING THE TABLE

Unlike singing and hearing the preaching of the Word, during which we welcome everyone in the room, this time of remembrance in the taking of the Lord's Supper is to be carefully reserved for believers with pure and repentant hearts, not to be taken lightly or without care. The apostle Paul wanted the church to take this corporate spiritual meal so seriously that he warned: "Whoever eats the bread or drinks the cup of the Lord in an unworthy manner will be guilty of sin against the body and blood of the Lord. Let a person examine himself; in this way let him eat the bread and drink from the cup. For whoever eats and drinks without recognizing the body, eats and drinks judgment on himself" (1 Cor. 11:27–29).

Jonathan Griffiths notes that Paul was addressing a peculiar manner of distasteful behavior occurring in the Corinthian church at the time. Wealthier Corinthian Christians would bring their own meal to the Lord's Table, even engaging in drunkenness, while the poor in their own church family would have nothing to eat. Clearly, remembering the broken body and shed blood of Christ was not their focus, and Paul called them to examine their hearts so that they would not partake in a manner unworthy of such a sacred meal. Griffiths adds: "But the application of the principle arguably extends more widely: it is possible to come to the Table without repenting of sin (especially those sins impacting relationships within the church), and so to participate 'unworthily.'"[6]

As believers, we should examine our own hearts before taking the Lord's Supper, and in that process focus on the kindness of God that leads to repentance. The church should see self-examination as a gift of grace. A pastor, elder, or church leader should see the process of administering the Lord's Supper to the church as an opportunity to minister to the congregation by pointing people to this practice. The process of walking people through the process of self-examination, confession, and repentance to protect the ordinance from being improperly taken is often referred to as "fencing the table." While the wording is undeniably exclusive, the bigger purpose is for the individuals of the church to look to Christ as Lord rather than being self-serving or indifferent. The fencing of the table helps ensure the ordinance does not become a lifeless ritual. Rather, every time it is taken, we aim for a true focus outside ourselves and on Christ.

We clarify our faith and salvation.

There is also an important missional component to fencing the table that presents itself in two different aspects. The first is *clarity regarding each participant's own faith and salvation*. It is a travesty to have someone sit in a church pew and take the Lord's Supper without it having any actual meaning to their lives due to being an unbeliever or a cultural Christian who is nonregenerate, a Christian in name only. A common practice at my church is for the pastor administering the Lord's Supper on a Sunday to state something like, "If you are here today and unsure about where you stand with the Lord, or perhaps not a

Christian, we are thrilled you are visiting today. But we want to let you know that this is a practice for the church. Rather than taking the elements today, we would love to see you take Christ." Then, the gospel will be explained again to the congregation. Fencing can also be an evangelistic opportunity.

(Side note: Within Christian circles, there are different views regarding whether a believer who is not a member of a specific church should take the Lord's Supper with them. I can understand those who reserve the Lord's Table for church members only if that church practices regenerate church membership, meaning part of the process of joining the church is ensuring one is a believer in the gospel and has had a Christian conversion.)

We witness to the community.

The other missional component is *the witness to the community.* How unfortunate to claim the name of Christ by taking the Lord's Supper and then walk out the door as if we have never heard the name of Jesus. If someone is tied to a church and its practices but lives a lifestyle antithetical to the church's witness and credibility to the world, "fencing the table" before administering the elements can at least allow a few moments of time for conviction and reflection to take place. It is important for believers to see it as an act of love and mission when careful parameters are put around the partaking of the Lord's Supper. It is easy to first be repelled or at least confused when an otherwise welcoming service is abruptly focused on an exclusive group of people. But that exclusive language points to the One who first gave us the ordinance, pointing us back to the God whose love and kindness are unlimited. The exclusive action points to the desire to include people not just in the ordinances but in the people of God and practice of the church. It is an invitation. Fencing leads to freedom.

Fencing leads to freedom.

EAT AND DRINK

When I was an elementary student, we walked forward to receive the elements during the Lord's Supper at my childhood church. My pastor would hold a large loaf of bread that he had broken in half while walking through the contents of the ordinance. Participants would tear off a piece of the bread and then dip it into a large cup of grape juice. My brother and I would always see who could grab the biggest piece of bread between the two of us. The pastor would often chuckle, knowing what mischief we were up to, as our mom rolled her eyes in line behind us. While I now can look back and see how that was inappropriate and immature, I would like to think that there's some tie-in there to childlike faith. I felt free to come to the Lord and take a big portion of the food at his table. I hope that now, rather than wanting the biggest piece of bread (still tempting), I will be mindful of the "bigness" of the gospel and the great lengths the Passover Lamb went in order to ensure God's promises are yes in my life and his church. The ordinance of the Lord's Supper helps me continue to believe.

DISCUSS AND REFLECT

1. What is an ordinance? Why are they important in the life of the church?

2. Why was the Passover important in the life of the people of Israel? How is Jesus the ultimate fulfillment of the Passover story from Exodus?

3. Why is fencing the table important for clarity and witness to the community?

4. Why is self-examination of the heart part of the taking of the Lord's Supper?

CHAPTER 7

Why Do We Baptize?

NOTHING IS MORE EXCITING than waking up on a Sunday morning when I know we will be celebrating baptisms at my local church. It is hard to express the joy and energy I feel when I get in the car and drive to church on those mornings. When someone steps into what we refer to as our baptismal tank, our church gets the privilege to participate as witnesses to what Jesus has ordained for the church to do: baptize believers.

Along with the Lord's Supper, the other ordinance Jesus gave to the church is baptism. At the end of the Gospel of Matthew, Jesus gave this calling to his followers, which is known as the Great Commission:

> "Go, therefore, and make disciples of all nations, baptizing them in the name of the Father and of the Son and of the Holy Spirit, teaching them to observe everything I have commanded you. And remember, I am with you always, to the end of the age." (Matt. 28:19–20)

Their calling from the Lord own's mouth was to go and make disciples. This is first evangelistic, as the call to baptize is tied to their going to the lost with the good news of salvation through Jesus Christ. Baptism should be seen as a starting point, where after one converts to Christianity through faith and repentance, they follow Jesus in obedience through baptism. It is appropriate to say that the church baptizes because Jesus commanded her to participate in this God-given ordinance.

THE PURPOSE OF BAPTISM

Baptism as an ordinance has two primary purposes in the life of the individual believer and the local church congregation.

Baptism provides a visible symbol of the work of the Spirit in one's life.

Baptism gives evidence of that which has resulted in one's faith in Jesus Christ and new birth. The visible portrait of going under the water through immersion, and then back out from the water, points to the invisible spiritual reality of one dying to sin and being made a new creation. It also identifies the person being baptized with the death, burial, and resurrection of Jesus

Christ. The act of baptism is a powerful picture of the story of the gospel. Common language one hears during a baptism is that the person going under the water is "buried with Christ in baptism and raised to walk in the newness of life."

At Pentecost, Peter gave his first sermon and declared the truth that "everyone who calls on the name of the Lord will be saved" (Acts 2:21). He went on to declare the reality of the resurrection, that indeed the risen Christ is the Messiah and Lord, and he indicted the Jewish people for their complicity in crucifying Christ. "When they heard this, they were pierced to the heart and said to Peter and the rest of the apostles, 'Brothers, what should we do?'" (v. 37). What an appropriate response when confronted with guilt before God! What do we do about this? What is our next step? Peter did not flinch and answered them: "Repent and be baptized, each of you, in the name of Jesus Christ for the forgiveness of your sins, and you will receive the gift of the Holy Spirit" (v. 38).

The call was to demonstrate the new saving faith by repenting of one's sins and getting baptized. Don't delay. Show your new allegiance to Jesus Christ, the one who saves.

Baptism is a public profession of faith in Jesus Christ. It allows the local church to corporately celebrate the work of the Spirit in the lives of new fellow believers in Jesus Christ. It is a type of public testimony before the church and the world that serves as a declaration of one's new association with Jesus

Christ. It is important to note that baptism does not forgive sins or bring about salvation. It is also not necessary for possessing a saving faith, since in the New Testament faith has always preceded baptism and is assumed, if not confirmed.

Baptism identifies the believer in the church body.

This is perhaps the least discussed component of baptism, but it is important and helpful to understand in the context of the local church and belonging to the body of Christ. Professor Stephen Wellum writes: "Baptism, then, is the defining mark of belonging, as well as a demarcation from the world (cf. Acts 2:40–41). Thus, in baptism, not only does Christ appropriate to himself the one who is baptized in his name and incorporate him into his body, but the person who is baptized also openly identifies with the Lord and his people."[1]

The New City Catechism states that baptism "is the washing with water in the name of the Father, the Son, and the Holy Spirit; it signifies and seals our adoption into Christ, our cleansing from sin, and our commitment to belong to the Lord and to his church."[2] The common baptism we hold together as fellow believers is a unifying bond and clear association of our belonging together as one body. We share "one Lord, one faith, one baptism, one God" (Eph. 4:5–6).

The fact that Jesus was baptized fascinated me as a kid. I couldn't help but think that I could actually do something Jesus himself did. I was sprinkled as an infant at my family's church and, before I came to true faith, it never occurred to me that baptism as Jesus commanded and modeled was also something for me. After my conversion to the Christian faith (upon hearing the gospel at a Fellowship of Christian Athletes retreat), I began reading my Bible and saw that Jesus was definitely baptized. If Jesus was baptized and he told us to go and baptize others, maybe I should get baptized too! It was mystifying though—Jesus had no sin to symbolize being buried or washed away. So why, then, was he baptized? Thankfully, Jesus tells us.

In Matthew 3, John the Baptist is shocked that the one he called the Lamb of God would want to be baptized by him. Jesus responded to his initial humble objection, stating: "Allow it for now, because this is the way for us to fulfill all righteousness" (v. 15). With Jesus's baptism, the people of God would get to see their Savior identify with them. In the same way water is seen as a sign of the judgment of God in the Scriptures (like the Genesis flood or Jonah being thrown into the storm-tossed sea), Jesus himself would receive that judgment. But unlike Jonah or those in the time of Noah, Jesus was without sin. He did not have a baptism of repentance like John or any other future baptized person. His baptism would declare him to be the true righteous One of Israel. Later, Jesus would claim: "I have a baptism to undergo, and how it consumes me until it is finished!" (Luke 12:50). He would take the plunge into death so that we could receive the everlasting waters of life.

John Piper helps us understand the baptized Christ by teaching that "Jesus saw his life as the fulfillment of all righteousness. The fact that participating in a baptism of repentance even though he had no sins to repent of is part of that shows that the righteousness he wanted to fulfill was the righteousness required not of himself, but of every sinful man." He goes on to say, "All the righteousness that would be required of men before the court of God, Jesus performed. So he joined fallen humanity, for whom he was providing righteousness by sharing their baptism."[3]

When Jesus came out of the water, the Father proclaimed in an audible voice that this was his son and he was pleased with him, and Jesus "saw the Spirit of God descending like a dove and coming down on him" (Matt. 3:16). The one who promised he would bring living water went into the water himself. The one in whom the Father is well pleased is the faithful Son. Jesus's baptism was a sign of his dedication to the Father, and our baptism, ordained by Christ, stands in the same loyalty. It is our public declaration of our new reality, presented righteous in Christ as faithful sons.

I went forward with baptism because I understood that since Jesus went into the depths for me, I can now live a resurrected life by his grace. As I considered baptism, I was still confused about why I had never been baptized outside of the sprinkling as an infant. A mentor at the time presented me with the question of the Ethiopian eunuch. The eunuch said, "Look, there's water. What would keep me from being baptized?" (Acts 8:36).

I didn't have an answer to the Ethiopian's question for myself. I was certainly a Christian who had had a conversion consisting of faith and repentance in response to hearing the gospel. The one objection I would have had prior to this would have been "I got baptized as a baby." But I now understood that the moment as an infant was a meaningful spiritual rite of passage for my Christian family, but it wasn't actually baptism. Because I was convinced that I had not been baptized like Jesus was and had no answer to what would keep me from getting baptized, I went forward with what I now know to be an ordinance given by Christ to the church for every believer. I got baptized.

When I recall the story of the Ethiopian eunuch, it seems evident that baptism should be seen as a starting point. By that I mean one does not have to be a Bible scholar or have every question answered—or even show signs of maturity—to receive the ordinance of baptism. The requirements to be baptized are faith and repentance. A church assuring that faith and repentance have occurred has the information needed for someone seeking to be baptized in the church. The responsibility of the person getting baptized, and the church performing the baptism, is to then carry out as a way of life the rest of the Great Commission and assure discipleship is happening and the baptized believer is being taught to observe everything Jesus commanded. This is the Great Commission Jesus gave, for people to be baptized into his life.

I once heard someone say that a church should not baptize someone that they have no intention to disciple. While I do believe there can be some nuance to that statement, there is wisdom in this line of thinking. Baptism is an act of the entire church and should be seen as a corporate, familial activity as one enters into life with God and his people.

Since baptism is evident in (1) the start of Jesus's public ministry, (2) the great calling and commission he gives to his disciples at the end of his earthly ministry, and (3) the call to repentance at Pentecost and beyond, it is clear that baptism is a critical component of the Christian story and a vital aspect of discipleship.

In Scripture, baptism takes place closely after conversion. But that does not mean that, if someone has been a Christian for an extended amount of time and hasn't been baptized, he should refuse to do so. A person's baptism testimony as a

Christian of numerous years can highlight the growing desire to follow the New Testament pattern and associate oneself with Christ and the church in the way the Savior ordained. One should not let pride (or fear that others may think the person wasn't priorly converted) keep one from baptism. It can be a tremendous encouragement to the church to see a long-standing, devoted believer get baptized. And it can help others see the importance of the ordinance in the Christian life. Just as Jesus taught us the gospel in words, he showed us the gospel through baptism. We proclaim the story of his death and resurrection when we step into the baptism waters, declaring our righteousness in him alone.

> Just as Jesus taught us the gospel in words,
> he showed us the gospel through baptism.

The ordinance of baptism points the church to the extraordinary: the miracle of a new creation found in the washing away of our sins. Church members should desire to see the baptismal at their church filled with water on a regular basis. Regular baptisms can be a sign of healthy life in a church as the Great Commission is being carried out. We pray that the Lord would continue to help us in making disciples and "baptizing them in the name of the Father and of the Son and of the Holy Spirit" (Matt. 28:19).

DISCUSS AND REFLECT

1. How does baptism tell the Christian story?

2. Baptism is a starting point. How does that shape your understanding of what is required to be baptized?

3. How does baptism display our allegiance to Christ and not this world?

CHAPTER 8

Why Do We Give?

EVER SINCE I FIRST read about him in the Bible, I have been intrigued by Barnabas from the book of Acts. His actual name is Joseph when we are first introduced to him in Acts 4, but he was given the nickname Barnabas, and this is how we see him referenced in the rest of the Bible. Acts tell us that Barnabas is translated "Son of Encouragement" (v. 36). Imagine being known as such an encouragement to others that it becomes your nickname. I can imagine some of the other disciples getting annoyed and yelling, "Enough already, say something negative!"

This great encourager first comes on the scene in the New Testament as the church is beginning to organize around the mission Jesus called them to in taking the gospel to those who have not heard. They were to be witnesses of the story of Jesus Christ crucified and risen, proclaiming, "There is salvation in no one else, for there is no other name under heaven given to people by which we must be saved" (v. 12).

After Peter and John were arrested for their words about the risen Jesus Christ, the disciples prayed for boldness to continue in their mission. Barnabas, who was apparently wealthy (based on his ownership of land), "sold a field he owned, brought the money, and laid it at the apostles' feet" (v. 37). An encourager, indeed! He saw the need and did what he could to help meet that need. He offered more than encouraging words. He gave self-sacrificial action.

At our church, we call finances "mission ammunition." But it is not merely up to the person who owns property and has disposable income to financially give to the mission of the church. Rather, every believer is to take part in giving of what they have. This is not just because there is a need (even though the need is large), but because Jesus cares about our hearts. Our hearts are directly tied to our bank accounts, "for where your treasure is, there your heart will be also" (Matt. 6:21). Financial assets are simultaneously a practical fuel that supports the mission of the church and the gateway into our hearts. God does not need our money to do what he wants to do. But he allows us to participate in laying down our own interests for the sake of the kingdom. If a church never talks about money, they are stating by their actions that they are not interested in your heart. What a terrible thing to say, even if indirectly!

The story following Barnabas's gift to the church in Acts 4 shows us how accurate Jesus's words were concerning the connection between our treasure and our hearts. After the great encourager's generosity, we are introduced to a married couple named Ananias and Sapphira (Acts 5:1). Like Barnabas, we are told they sold a piece of property. But unlike Barnabas, Ananias "kept back part of the proceeds with his wife's knowledge, and brought a portion of it and laid it at the apostles' feet" (v. 2).

This may seem like no big deal upon first hearing the story. They gave money, after all. But the disciples saw things differently.

> "Ananias," Peter asked, "why has Satan filled your heart to lie to the Holy Spirit and keep back part of the proceeds of the land? Wasn't it yours while you possessed it? And after it was sold, wasn't it at your disposal? Why is it that you planned this thing in your heart? You have not lied to people but to God." (vv. 3–4)

Seeing Barnabas make a generous contribution from the entire proceeds of his field, Ananias and Sapphira may have wanted to look spiritual themselves in selling their property and giving money to the church. Maybe they would get their own nicknames like Barnabas. I hate to ruin the story if you haven't heard it, but within a few verses, both of them are dead. It can be a jarring passage. The moral of the story is not that everyone needs to give to the church 100 percent of the proceeds they make from any sale or commission, but rather that Barnabas made the contribution willingly from his heart, whereas Ananias and his wife were acting secretively out of greed or a desire to seem more generous than they were truly willing to be. Ultimately, this married couple had issues of the heart. Barnabas did not need to show himself as spiritual or impressive; he was acting out of the overflow of his heart.

When Paul was writing to the Corinthian church about generosity, it was all linked to what Jesus had already done in their hearts through their salvation, reminding them that we thank God for the indescribable gift he has given us in the gospel (2 Cor. 9:15). Since God has lavished us with grace, our posture is one of open hands due to a transformed heart. God provides and every resource in the universe is, and always has been, his.

The opposite posture is to be closefisted, believing that all is for our own consumption. Christians must realize that nothing is truly ours; God owns "the cattle on a thousand hills" (Ps. 50:10). This is why generosity in the local church context is often referred to as stewardship. We don't own a single thing. Rather, we are stewards. What a joy to receive blessings that we steward in our lives for God and give back to his mission.

I assume that none of us have been prompted to give of our resources a greater thing than Abraham, whom God asked to sacrifice his long-awaited son, Isaac. After Abraham's faith was tested and proved to be steadfast, God provided a ram to be sacrificed instead. Reflecting on this, the late theologian A. W. Tozer wrote in his book *The Pursuit of God*:

> After that bitter and blessed experience I think the words "my" and "mine" never had again the same meaning for Abraham. The sense of possession which they connote was gone from his heart. . . . There can be no doubt that this possessive clinging to things is one of the most harmful habits in the life. Because it is so natural it is rarely recognized for the evil that it is; but its outworkings are tragic. We are often hindered from giving up our treasures to the Lord out of fear for their safety; this is especially true when those treasures are loved relatives and friends. But we need have no such fears. Our Lord came not to destroy but to save. Everything we commit to Him, and nothing is really safe which is not so committed.[1]

The chapter where these words are found is rightly titled "The Blessedness of Possessing Nothing." We should think of ourselves as living a life that is rented. That eternal perspective helps us see ourselves not as owners, but as stewards of what we have been given.

HOW MUCH?

So, if one has accepted this and is willing to participate, a common and understandable question is: How much am I supposed to give? We can begin to grasp our place in generosity by what Paul wrote to the Corinthian church, that "each person should do as he has decided in his heart—not reluctantly or out of compulsion, since God loves a cheerful giver" (2 Cor. 9:7). The question Paul is prodding us to ask ourselves is, *How is my heart?* The answer (according to Jesus's linking our heart to our treasure) will involve more than generosity, but certainly not less. If I am not willing to be generous, there is something amiss in my heart.

I also find it fascinating that Paul gives us a window into the heart of God by telling us what he loves. God loves generosity. A generous spirit is a reflection of himself, the greatest Giver of all, who loved us so fully that he gave his only Son. Jesus, likewise, who gave his life, points us not to a literal percentage of our earnings and income, but rather to an overarching posture of generosity.

I had a conversation with my uncle, who is a generous Christian, asking about a common pattern in the Old Testament of giving a tithe. Since God is our greatest treasure, he stated, why would we think anything less than what was prescribed in the Old Testament would be appropriate for us living in the new covenant today? The literal tithe might not be required today in the same way it was under the Mosaic law, but it does not for a moment suggest we should hoard our possessions. My uncle stated that by his conviction, the Old Testament tithe is a starting point, especially for those living in the West, who have means incomprehensible to much of the world. It can be easy to think that generous giving is for those who happen to have plenty to give, but Jesus seemed to anticipate that train of thought:

> Sitting across from the temple treasury, he watched how the crowd dropped money into the treasury. Many rich people were putting in large sums. Then a poor widow came and dropped in two tiny coins worth very little. Summoning his disciples, he said to them, "Truly I tell you, this poor widow has put more into the treasury than all the others.

> For they all gave out of their surplus, but she out of her poverty has put in everything she had—all she had to live on." (Mark 12:41–44)

The rich people were putting in a lot of money. I can imagine the feelings of the woman, whom we are told was a poor widow, as she walked up and placed a mere two coins into the bucket. I can't help but wonder if it made a shallow echo sound when it hit the bottom. Yet Jesus consistently sees our finances as an issue of the heart, and here he could see the hearts of all parties. The wealthy people who put in large sums of money gave out of their abundance. They had some extra cash that would not affect their way of life if they gave it. These people likely would not notice the money was not in their pockets anymore. But the woman had a different story. She gave all she had. The conclusion is not "go and do likewise," but rather to see that, in God's economy, the manner in which we give is more important to the condition of our hearts than the total sum of the money.

TRUSTED STEWARDS

Generous church members should make up a generous church. In other words, the church itself should be generous with what it has received. Since we believe the Great Commission is our highest calling as a church, we give generously outside of our church walls so the gospel can be carried to the ends of the earth. One primary way we do this is through giving to trusted programs that send and support international missionaries and church planters here in North America. It is our responsibility to fuel the mission through Great Commission giving. Believers corporately are "commanded to support those who preach the gospel (Matt. 10:10; Luke 10:7; 1 Cor. 9:6–14; 1 Tim. 5:17–18)."[2] We are also called to help the poor among us. When church members give to their church, it should mean they know those resources are providing the things needed for that church to operate and flourish locally, to join in funding the Great Commission across the world, to support those in need within the congregation through benevolence ministry, and to partner with local trusted organizations providing needs for the community.

Generous church members should
make up a generous church.

The God who saved us from our sins cares about guarding our hearts. Our faithfulness matters to him. Money can easily become an idol and rise to such prominence in one's life that it controls every decision they make. It is not uncommon to hear or see how money ruined a relationship or completely changed someone's personality and what matters to them. But money is not the problem. The love of money is the problem. The Scriptures say that "the love of money is a root of all kinds of evil, and by craving it, some have wandered away from the faith and pierced themselves with many griefs" (1 Tim. 6:10).

> But money is not the problem. The love of money is the problem.

God does not want his children to settle for lesser loves. One, because he will not share his glory with anyone or anything else (Isa. 42:8), and two, because he knows what disordered affections can do to someone. As Paul says, this love and craving of money caused some to leave the faith and others to have many griefs. The money Barnabas used to be an encourager is the same that caused Ananias to act out of his own interests. The difference is that Barnabas had money, but money had Ananias. The love of money is evil, not money itself.

So, how do we guard ourselves from this?

Pray for and carry out generosity. While there are numerous organizations and places to practice generosity that are worthy and right, it only makes sense that the local church be the primary and greatest place of your giving. God has given the greatest mission to the church, and this is where disciples are made and the place from which they are sent. The ammunition for mission and the training ground for the forming of our hearts primarily belongs to the church. Joining a local church gives us the incredible privilege of being part of opening our hands as stewards of God's resources, to join his people in demonstrating that the Lord is our greatest treasure. We give to our church because we love the One who "first loved us" (1 John 4:19). We thank God for his indescribable gift of our salvation in Jesus Christ (2 Cor. 9:15).

The next time you are in church, and the offering plates pass or the online giving link comes up on a screen, consider that the church leaders are providing this opportunity for the purity of your heart. And give cheerfully, as the Lord smiles upon that.

DISCUSS AND REFLECT

1. Why is it important to see money as mission ammunition? What does this mean?

2. God sees us as a steward of the resources he has given us. How does that truth shape your understanding of generosity?

3. How can you keep yourself from the love of money?

4. In God's economy, the portion is more important than the sum. How does the story of the woman with the two coins help us to understand generosity in the eyes of God?

5. Why should the church be the first recipient of our generosity?

CHAPTER 9

Why Do We Evangelize?

SOMETIMES I AM ASKED whether my local church is "geared more toward believers or unbelievers." What the person is wondering is whether our church is more focused on evangelism or discipleship, with the assumption that a church usually emphasizes one over the other. But in the depiction of the church in the New Testament, as well as the gospel stories of Jesus and the apostles, the two practices of evangelism and discipleship are linked together. I tell our church regarding this matter that when we share our faith with someone, we are pointing them not merely to a *decision* to believe in Jesus, but also inviting them into *life with God*. Discipleship is essential and should begin in the local church as soon as one is converted to new life in Christ. The question, however, is: What, exactly, are we discipling them toward?

Hopefully, the answer to that question lands somewhere in the context of becoming more like Jesus. When Jesus was questioned about why he spent time with tax collectors and sinners, he responded by telling the stories of the lost sheep and the lost coin (Luke 15:1–10). He resonated with his agrarian audience when he reminded them that if they lost one sheep, they would leave the other ninety-nine to go and find just one who had gotten away. That one lost sheep mattered enough to leave the other ninety-nine who were not lost in order to bring the one home. Framing the same principle a different way, Jesus went on to remind them that if a silver coin was lost, they would search as long as it took to find that coin and then rejoice when the coin was found. Jesus claimed that angels rejoice when one sinner repents and comes to faith in Christ. Let me say that again: the angels rejoice when a lost person is found!

I often lose my wallet and cell phone. (Apparently, there are apps to help you with such problems, but I'm not too caught up in these advancements.) When my wallet or phone goes missing, I retrace every step imaginable. I call the coffee shop where I was earlier that day and take steps with my head down, searching my entire office. Those are valuable items for me. I need to find them. How much greater in value is a human soul who was lost and is now found, brought from death to life and into a relationship with Jesus Christ? That is the point Jesus is trying to make. The ninety-nine sheep never lost their value, but when one was lost, the focus shifted.

The local church should care for the ninety-nine sheep, but they cannot neglect the one who is lost. I want to pastor a church that gets excited about what Jesus and the angels do. Church leaders and members alike should see evangelism as a significant function of their church because it is the primary ministry we are given here on earth. Sadly, churches that focus on "seekers" can get a bad rap: people assume that must mean the church waters down the message of the Bible and fails to take discipleship of existing believers seriously.

This is an unfortunate attitude. A church that is not taking the Bible seriously (by belittling evangelism or discipleship) is a church that *is* neglecting the ninety-nine *and* failing to prioritize the lost one. But it does not have to be this way. What reaches the lost sheep is not a minimized version of the gospel, but the actual truth of Jesus Christ crucified and risen. It is commonly said in evangelical circles that "what you win someone *with*, you win them *to*." Meaning, if you reach someone with something other than the message of faith in Jesus Christ and repentance of sin, you have reached them to something other than biblical Christianity. You don't need a beginner gospel to reach people, and you don't need an advanced gospel to keep people. If your church preaches the Bible clearly and loves the lost passionately, you are part of a church that resembles the life of Christ.

You don't need a beginner gospel to
reach people, and you don't need an
advanced gospel to keep people.

If Jesus told us he came to seek and save the lost, and discipleship is becoming more like Jesus every day, a local church that does not emphatically care about reaching the lost is missing the mark. Church members must be reminded that they are to live on mission in their local contexts and see their church model the same goal. I am intrigued when churches full of great Bible teaching and sound doctrine do not emphasize the need to reach the lost and do not position themselves to try to do such. I want the theology and doctrine to which we hold strongly as a church to fuel our mission into our community. We send our members because Jesus has sent us. Jesus said, "As you sent me into the world, I also have sent them into the world" (John 17:18).

LAST WORDS

Last words traditionally carry a great deal of weight. Farewell addresses become written in history as significant, and words from leaders on their deathbeds have become legendary in certain cultures. I know stories of parents who were diagnosed with terminal illness and were able to record final words to the children to be treasured forever. Last words matter. And the greater the status or relationship of the one departing, the greater the importance of their last words. Jesus "is before all things, and by him all things hold together" (Col. 1:17). Everything he says or does carries the weight of eternity. And Jesus has last recorded words after his resurrection and before his ascension. Three years of pouring his life into his disciples and he leaves them with a clear calling.

These are the last recorded words of Jesus in the Gospel of Matthew:

> "All authority has been given to me in heaven and on earth. Go, therefore, and make disciples of all nations, baptizing them in the name of the Father and of the Son and of the Holy Spirit, teaching them to observe everything I have commanded you. And remember, I am with you always, to the end of the age." (28:18–20)

These are the last recorded words of Jesus in the Gospel of Luke:

> "This is what is written: The Messiah will suffer and rise from the dead the third day, and repentance for forgiveness of sins will be proclaimed in his name to all the nations, beginning at Jerusalem. You are witnesses of these things. And look, I am sending you what my Father promised. As for you, stay in the city until you are empowered from on high." (24:46–49)

These are the last recorded words of Jesus in the book of Acts before his ascension:

> "But you will receive power when the Holy Spirit has come on you, and you will be my witnesses in Jerusalem, in all Judea and Samaria, and to the ends of the earth." (1:8)

Clearly the disciples were trained to be sent. This was the point.

More than two thousand years later, the call upon the followers of Jesus remains: we are his witnesses. But unfortunately, discipleship as it can be practiced today can make the mission "out of sight, out of mind." The process of growing in discipleship can mean nothing more than receiving information. It is too easy for the outcome to be more knowledgeable

Christians, the ninety-nine just sticking together and being fed all day.

It is simultaneously life-giving and sad for me to see brand-new believers often as the most passionate evangelists. They are excited about being found and grateful for the grace of God in their lives, and they want their friends and family who do not know the Lord to know about the life-changing message of salvation. But if that flame is not fanned by more mature Christians, these new believers can settle into a Christian subculture where they are only learning about (and not sharing) their faith. The transition from excited new convert to studious disciple removed from culture does not have to be inevitable.

But if that flame is not fanned by more mature Christians, these new believers can settle into a Christian subculture where they are only learning about (and not sharing) their faith.

The local church should want to see believers grow not only in knowledge of Christ, but in his *likeness* as well. Jesus still leaves the ninety-nine to find the one today, and the church should have their flashlights lit searching for that missing silver coin. Please hear me: this does not come at the cost of solid theology or biblical disciplines. In fact, it depends on solid theology and biblical disciplines. Compromise in lifestyle and doctrine will not reach anyone with the true gospel of Christ.

GROW AND GO

Mature Christians follow Jesus into the world. The Pharisees who questioned him were certainly knowledgeable, but they were not in step with the way of Christ. It caused them to push back on the very thing they should be celebrating. Instead, "the Pharisees and scribes were complaining, 'This man welcomes sinners and eats with them'" (Luke 15:2). I do not believe any local church intentionally neglects the lost, or believes they do, even if it happens in practice. But actions speak louder than words, and we can see what a person or organization values by where they give their time and resources.

Churches should "send." Since there are lost sheep and lost coins, all church members should see themselves as missionaries in their local community. As church leaders model and encourage this posture toward the world, church members can grow in Christlike discipleship. It can be difficult to understand how to live life as a missionary when one does not have a passport in hand with plans to move overseas. But the life of a local missionary begins by having the mindset that it is exactly how Jesus wants you to be and then to open your eyes to the opportunities right in front of you to share Christ with neighbors, family members, classmates, coworkers, and friends who do not know the Lord. An invitation to church is also a helpful tool in ministry to others locally, so they can see what your faith is about and why the local church is so significant in your life. It is also helpful to take advantage of any evangelism training your local church provides. Paul reminded believers in the New Testament book of Romans that "faith comes from what is heard, and what is heard comes through the message about Christ" (10:17). Our faith is to be shared, and it is to be heard. The results of whether it is *received* are in the hands of our sovereign God.

So, what does it look like for a church to care about the lost? For our local church it means three primary things.

Our faith is to be shared, and it is to be heard. The results of whether it is *received* are in the hands of our sovereign God.

Sending is part of our congregational language and DNA.

If you are a member of our church, you regularly hear stories of those being sent locally and globally. In being sent locally, we are convinced that ministry happens in the home (where parents have the responsibility of raising their children in the truth of Christ), at work, at school, and in social circles—basically, anywhere a believer regularly goes. The routine presence of a disciple of Jesus Christ should positively impact any place. In fact, I am convinced that if members of local churches thought prayerfully and strategically about their workplaces and on their campuses about their witness for Christ, it could have a tremendous impact on not only individual communities, but society as a whole.

We refer to this strategic mindset for the person in the professional setting as being "called, not employed."[1] For those who are students, we say "called, not enrolled." In the professional realm, this means that Christians do not just see their jobs as merely a place to provide for the family, achieve career ambitions, secure benefits, and save for retirement. As important as all those aspects of working certainly are, the Christian is left with the important task of representing Christ and the church as a missionary. Every time a believer pulls into the parking garage in his place of employment, he has a calling beyond being a nurse, a teacher, an accountant, or a salesperson; that calling is to be like Christ and point others to him.

This mindset also allows jobs that may seem mundane or less than ideal to still carry meaning. Paul instructed the Colossians: "Whatever you do, in word or in deed, do everything in the name of the Lord Jesus, giving thanks to God the Father through him" (Col. 3:17). Many college students work part-time retail jobs that they do not see as relevant for their future careers. But every person working beside them or coming in as a customer is made in the image of God. The work may not seem "relevant," but the calling itself is relevant everywhere. Church members see their part of their local church's story when they see themselves as being called, and not employed.

We encourage stay-at-home mothers to see themselves as called to their children and their peers in the same season of life. We have seen ladies in our church take tremendous acts of intentionality in connecting with other stay-at-home mothers who do not know the Lord. I regularly hear stories of church members organizing lunches, dinners, book clubs, and other avenues of cultivating relationships with coworkers, all based on the desire to share Christ and his church with them. This is not a bait-and-switch type approach to get a notch on the belt of conversion, but out of a true calling to be missionaries where God has placed them.

We consider the unbeliever on Sunday morning.

This is where it can get dicey if you don't have a missionary mindset. At our church, we believe the gathering is mainly for believers and, even more so, church members. But we also want the guests, especially the lost sheep, to be considered and valued when they are brought to a service by a church member. This means we want the atmosphere to be friendly and any programming to be executed well. Excellence is an important value we strive for because we believe we are stewards of the calling and opportunity God has given us as a local church. Excellence is not defined by a style and should not detract from substance, but it means we do the best we can to provide a hospitable environment for the person making a big decision to walk into the doors of a church. If they have children, we want them to see a children's ministry that is clean, safe, and enjoyable for their child. The music played during the service should not seem thrown together at the last minute. The greeters should be warm and strategically placed to assist guests. Even the bathrooms should not be hard to find.

What some may view as pragmatism is merely hospitality. When it comes to the sermon, we want to make sure the preaching is understood by all. I think about the person who has been a Christian for longer than I have been alive, as well as the person who is visiting a church for the first time in their lives. My hope is that both of those individuals can leave the service understanding what was preached that day. Any size church with any style and any level of financial resources can attempt to do things well—be hospitable and be clear.

Any size church with any style and any level of financial resources can attempt to do things well—be hospitable and be clear.

We work to earn and keep the trust of our members.

Considering guests for our church means making sure we have the trust of our members; they need to know they can "safely" invite their friends to a church service. In our cynical and unforgiving society, second chances are rarely given. I am convinced that other than the rare exception of experiencing a traumatic life event, an unbeliever is not coming to church for any reason whatsoever. I feel bad sometimes for churches who believe that if they just change their music style or do a catchy sermon series, unbelievers will flock through the doors. While I appreciate sincere effort to reach an unbelieving community and believe it is the stuff angels care about it, why would someone who isn't a Christian care that there are guitars instead of a pipe organ? That person may actually like a pipe organ! But even so, it likely will not get the person to give church a try.

I still have not met the unbeliever who heard the pastor dresses trendy and the drummer is elite, so they decided to go to church. One thing *can* get an unbeliever to come to church, though, and that is the invitation and arm of a trusted friend. Our church leaders understand that fellow members of our local church are regularly investing their lives into their unbelieving friends and would not invite them to a church service they secretly are not enthusiastic about themselves. Loving the Lord and believing the gospel will get someone to want to share their lives and faith with a friend. But unless they love their church, inviting the friend to join them is not happening. I would be mortified if I knew church members did not want to invite their friends to our church. I think it would cause me to reevaluate everything I am doing in ministry. This should not mean church members expect perfection. It should mean they are joining a church they believe in so much that they cannot wait to have their non-Christian friend join them.

THE DOUBLE PROMISE

Among our leaders, we hold to a value we call the "double promise." This consists of two commitments, which we strive toward every Sunday on behalf of our people. We want there to be:

1. No disclaimer required to your friend on the way to church.

    By no disclaimer, we mean that we never want there to be a heads-up about something weird, troubling, or awkward the visitor will experience. An example would be, "Hey, I am so glad you are coming with me today, but I just want you to know that the pastor is a good guy and means well, but he can go off on political rants sometimes. Just know he doesn't mean any harm by it." Or, "I know you're an introvert, but they like to have new people stand up and say their names." If you invite someone to your church, the last thing you should be doing is giving disclaimers on the drive there.

2. No apology on the drive home.

    Our sincere goal is that you do not have to give any apology on our behalf when you leave the service. No "I'm sorry the kids ministry was so chaotic. I have no idea what happened," or "I've never heard the music sound so awful. I'm sorry your ears are ringing; it won't be like that next time."

We want the members of our church to know they can invite their unchurched friends to our services, and—apart from the invasive work of the Holy Spirit—they will not experience anything awful. We have certainly messed this up before. It is a sad day when we realize we've committed a "double promise" violation, not because we believe the kingdom of God hinges on how we approach and execute a Sunday morning at our church, but because our members are leaving the ninety-nine to go and find the one, and the people making leadership decisions concerning how Sunday morning feels and functions should not be a hindrance in their inviting a friend to church. People come to church on the arm of a trusted friend, and that trusted friend must trust their church. If church members are to be sent, they should have a clear place to run back with the sheep who just might be found.

> People come to church on the arm of a trusted friend, and that trusted friend must trust their church.

REMEMBER YOUR STORY

If church members desire to be growing in their faith, it will not be at the neglect of what Jesus has called us to do and be as his missionaries. When we follow Christ into the world and join him in being a friend of sinners, we are remembering the power of the gospel in a manner that goes outside ourselves. We are also being for others what God, in his grace, allowed someone else to be for us, prior to our conversion. Someone was the mouthpiece of the message. I encourage our church members regularly to remember the name of the person who first shared Christ with them and never to lose sight of the compassionate and courageous act that person did to point them to the good news. It is hard to neglect the lost when you remember that someone refused to neglect you.

I do believe that sending begins with church members at the local level who see themselves as missionaries for Christ and representatives of their local churches in the community. But of course, if we are going to respond to the call of Christ to go to the ends of the earth, we must also participate in missions globally. In the next chapter, we will look at why church members should have an active global vision they participate in with and for their church.

DISCUSS AND REFLECT

1. Why is remembering your own story important in developing and maintaining a heart for the lost?

2. Mature believers follow Jesus into the world. Why did he claim this? What is it that keeps people from seeing a heart for the lost as a Christian maturity issue?

3. How can you and your church create a culture of evangelism and make it a priority like Jesus did? Does your church seem more interested in the ninety-nine sheep or the one that is missing? How about you?

CHAPTER 10

Why Do We Send Missionaries?

I ONCE HAD A sincere church member come to me with a fair question. He asked me why, as a church, we give such a large sum of money overseas and push for people to move their lives across the world as full-time missionaries when there are unbelievers and significant needs in our own city that seem never to disappear. That was a question from his heart; he was not being critical. He truly wanted to know why we seemed to be bypassing our own city to send financial resources and people to other cities for ministry.

This is not a unique encounter. It can be hard to grasp why money, time, and people can go elsewhere when people see the needs in front of their eyes locally. The quick answer I wanted to give was that we want to be about missions both locally and globally. While that is true, there is more to the story.

I once had the same thought pattern. I thought mission trips were a great thing and admired people who responded to a calling upon their lives to go full-time into global missions, but I did not understand the need to do such a thing when there were unbelievers in our own community who still had not been reached. I then had a conversation with a friend from my high school days, who lives full-time with her family as a missionary overseas with the International Mission Board. She affirmed that, yes, there are unbelievers still to be reached in my community, but she pivoted to softly rebuking me that there is a major difference between my unbelieving neighbor and someone living in a largely unreached nation elsewhere on earth. She reminded me that where I live, people at least have *access* to the gospel. There seems to be a church on every corner, and there are several Christian music and talk shows on the radio. One is not far removed at work, school, or in the neighborhood from someone who would claim to be Christian. It does not mean they are necessarily hearing the gospel, but they are nearer to hearing the good news of Jesus than others.

Missionaries being sent globally are often strategically headed to places with no access to the message of Jesus Christ in the city or, at times, the entire nation. It is a matter of taking the gospel to where it has not been heard. When put that way, it clicked for me, and our church has never looked back as our elders agreed together that we wanted to be a sending church. Our local church is committed to sending people and resources to underreached areas where access to the gospel is limited or nonexistent. We do not do this alone, but we do it wholeheartedly.

I tell our church that when it comes to the local needs of ministry, *we* are here. This is our community. Our church *meets* inside our city, and a vast majority of our members *live* inside our city. In some cities, there is little or no evangelical presence. My local church is not in one of those places. Far too many cities and villages across the world do not even have a Bible in the language of the people. As church members, we get to do something about this by being senders. This is an active strategy and cultivation of our church to raise up missionaries to take the gospel where it needs to be heard.

GOERS AND SENDERS

One couple in our church has traveled the world on various mission trips and continues to do so, but they have chosen not to leave the United States as residents and have rooted themselves in their church and community. They will also tell you that the Lord has placed a clear call to international missions on their lives. How can this be since they have no plans to move overseas? They believe that their calling as laypeople is to be senders. This means they build relationships with those in our church who are sensing a type of desire or calling to be global missionaries. They also lead classes about global missions and help our church think strategically about the Great Commission and how we can fulfill our desire to be a sending church. While every church member might not have the exact calling as these two, all church members can and should see themselves as goers or as senders. We all play a part as local church members.

Senders

Most people will likely not move overseas as full-time missionaries. (Though there might be more people open to the possibility than we realize.) Short-term trips can help clarify a calling and kindle a flame for the unreached people of the nations. As your church prioritizes global missions through giving, short-term trips, and long-term sending, it is important to see how you play a part in the sending focus as a church member.

Pray. The commitment to pray is an underrated and critical component of having a sending role as a church member. In Luke 10:2, Jesus told his disciples to pray for laborers in the harvest. Our congregation partners with a network of churches in which the pastors and ministry leaders all set our phone alarms to go off at 10:02 a.m. each day. This is a reminder for us to pray what Jesus commanded us to in Luke 10:2 and ask the Lord to send more missionaries into the field from our churches. Joining in this daily prayer is an easy step any church member can take to be a part of global sending at your church.

Give. It is important to mention the financial aspect of missions again. A church member who gives generously to the local church is functioning as a sender (assuming the church has properly built a habit of giving to global missions). The last thing we want for a missionary is to worry about finances. These people are choosing to move their families across the world for the Great Commission and are doing so from our churches. Sending missionaries into the global field is extremely expensive. This is a major burden for one church to carry, let alone the family going! This is a primary reason we work in a network of churches, combining resources together with like-minded sister congregations to take the gospel to the world. I am a firm believer that we can do much more together than we ever could apart. If your church is part of a denomination or network of churches, see that first as a global missions partnership for the Great Commission. A group of churches financially partnering together for missions is putting feet onto the Luke 10:2 prayer and catapults laborers into the harvest from like-minded churches.

Commit. Another way we send is by helping people make strategic decisions for their lives based on the mission of God. We certainly need people to root their lives in our own city and help us reach our community for Christ, but there are cities in our own nation with limited access to evangelical churches. An answer to this need has been a strong focus on church planting during the twenty-first century. Networks of churches are planting churches in cities across America in need of an evangelical presence.

If there is one thing a church plant needs to get going and have an impact in their new community, it is people. A sending church is not afraid to ask members to consider moving somewhere for the maximum kingdom impact through the local church. Being a part of a church plant in a highly underchurched city is a missionary endeavor. In a society where working remotely is commonplace and many jobs are transferable, people can be an answer to a Luke 10:2 prayer by considering moving to be part of a church plant their home church is involved with supporting. Church members who live out their membership are critical for the flourishing of a church plant, as church plants ideally reach and connect with people who are not Christians.

Church members who live out their membership are critical for the flourishing of a church plant.

A sending church encourages church members to leverage their life phase for the kingdom of God. For some, it may mean being a present family in your suburban subdivision where you own a home and your kids are in school, and for others it might mean that you can be a nurse on a hospital floor or teach second grade and rent an apartment anywhere in America. Why not leverage where you are now in life for maximum kingdom impact? Whenever we have a church member who moves out of our city because of work, college, family transition, or any other basic reason that causes one to relocate, the mindset of our church is that we are sending that person to go be a great church member in their next city and church.

One of our church elders had a breakthrough moment in his faith as a young man early in his career. He realized that he did not need a paycheck from a church to have a ministry. This realization happened long before he became a lay elder in our church, but this has allowed him to see himself as involved in cultivating a love for the Great Commission in others and to leverage his career as a business owner for the work of the local church. He has the ministry of being a sender simply by believing he has a ministry that does not require a church business card or staff bio on a website. He is quick to sign up for short-term trips, and he is consistent as an elder in his desire to see our church's giving toward the Great

Commission increase annually. Every church member can be part of the Great Commission as a sender through their local church.

> Whenever we have a church member who moves out of our city because of work, college, family transition, or any other basic reason that causes one to relocate, the mindset of our church is that we are sending that person to go be a great church member in their next city and church.

Goers

One fall afternoon at Starbucks, I sat down with one of our pastors. I was a little nervous about the conversation because I had never told someone before that I believed they were called to global missions. Since I am not the Holy Spirit, and I was also telling someone I worked with that he needed to go somewhere else, I was sweating a little walking into the meeting. How would he receive the senior pastor telling him he should move across the world? I did not want him to take it as me not wanting him here. In fact, I think so much of him that I believed we would be sending our best as a missionary to the world. After some chitchat, I finally began what I wanted to share with him, using the classic awkward conversation starter: "So . . ."

I told him that I thought he and his wife should start praying about global missions. I then gave my heartfelt disclaimer that I loved him being part of the team and that he was doing an amazing job as one of our pastors. I braced myself for the startled reply of a husband and father of two school-aged children that I just told to pray about moving them across the world where there might not even be a Starbucks. He smiled and said, "Funny you should say that; we have been praying about global missions for our family." I was floored. God was clearly up to something. The process began, and this family pursued the next steps of their calling to move their family to another country as full-time missionaries. One of the highlights of my ministry life was attending their official commissioning and sending ceremony after they completed their training. This was the first time we had officially sent members of our own church overseas full-time.

During that Starbucks meeting, I knew God was orchestrating something, but I thought it was about this one specific family. But it was this staff family's willingness to leave the familiarity of our church (and our willingness to send them) that lit a mission fire in our church. Since their sending, we have had several church members apply for passports—not to take a vacation, but to move overseas because of the Great Commission. There is now even an expectation that we will have a sending commissioning every year from our church. It just took one family saying they would go. We then saw someone from our executive leadership team leave behind everything she knew and move across the ocean to be part of a church plant in a global city.

We call these sending times of our great friends and ministry partners "gospel goodbyes." Our elders have increased our financial support for global missions. It is now part of the air we breathe as a church. It is important that church members see financial support and sending as the business of the church. Exposure to the field through short-term trips and partnering with existing missionaries and organizations is a fantastic way for churches to take next steps and for members to engage in the Great Commission outside of their communities.

If you feel called to go, speak to leaders in your church and pursue next steps. Many churches are members of networks that facilitate training, evaluation, placement, and support. And church leaders, if one of your own approaches with a desire to go, as much as it may hurt to say a gospel goodbye, take seriously their desire and help them take effective next steps, knowing that "labor in the Lord is not in vain" (1 Cor. 15:58).

Most importantly, every member of a local church can and should be supportive and proactive in having a global focus. It is easy to think like the church member who asked me why we put resources into ministry outside our city, and I can understand because I was once wary about it myself. Now I know that we send because Jesus sent, and he continues to send to where his gospel has never been heard. We must care about the nations as church members because Jesus cares about the nations. I have seen a global focus also impact ministry locally. I have had hard conversations with people who are quick to sign up for a short-term mission trip but never seem to think about the lost locally. People soon realize the inconsistency and gain confidence, knowing that if they can talk to someone about the Lord in a nation across the globe, they can have a conversation with a coworker.

> We must care about the nations as church members because Jesus cares about the nations.

A global focus impacts every area of the local church. Our commitment to global missions fuels from the conviction that the gospel must get to the unreached before they face God's just judgment for their sins. We want to see the message of his redeeming love extended to where one day there will be no unreached people. This happens with one church at a time playing its part in the Great Commission. The good news is that the Lord will be with you every step of the way. Jesus says to his people, "And remember, I am with you always, to the end of the age" (Matt. 28:20).

DISCUSS AND REFLECT

1. Why is having a heart for global missions an important aspect of the life of the church?

2. If moving overseas isn't in your plans, what are the ways you can participate in global missions through your church? What aspects of being a sender excite you?

3. The book mentioned the mindset of wondering why money is spent on global missions when there are needs in your own community. How would you respond to that question?

4. How can you develop a mindset of being a sender in your local church?

CONCLUSION

A Plea from the Heart Regarding the Local Church

ANY WRITER'S "PLEA" IN the context of Christian social media, articles, or books these days seems to be a plea to the church. Whether the call is for the church to rediscover her New Testament roots, or purify herself, or to be less political, there is no shortage of church critiques and callouts. It is fair to say it has become a cottage industry. While I am not going to pretend all is fine and the church doesn't need regular renewal, Jesus sees his church differently than we often do. Jesus sees the church as his bride, a bride he has chosen for himself and has washed to present without spot or blemish. Who can claim to be without spot or blemish? Not me! I'm guessing you can't either. Jesus can. In fact, he is the only one who ever lived a perfect life. The good news is that his perfect righteousness is given to his bride at our salvation, and because of that amazing act of grace, you can claim status as the bride

Jesus describes. He has made her spotless by cleansing her with his blood. Which now means, in Christ, we can claim to be without spot or blemish. That is our spiritual status before the Lord (Eph. 5:27)!

Jesus loves the church and has gone to great lengths to purify her for himself. I want to love what Jesus loves. At face value, that is not a controversial statement. It sounds like a fitting aspiration for a person claiming to be a follower of Jesus Christ. Most Christians I know would agree with that statement. But the agreement seems to quickly halt when the object of that love is the church. Imagine for a moment, if you're a husband reading this, that I told you I liked you a lot, but I don't think much of your wife. In fact, I enjoy when we spend time together, but I want nothing to do with your wife. So let's just allow me and you to hang out. I'm just going to guess that wouldn't go over well. I might even need to ice the black eye you gave me afterward.

Similarly, if you claim to like Jesus but not his bride, or are merely indifferent toward her, it is a relationship that is not going to work because it is a relationship with a Jesus you have invented. So my plea isn't really to the church. It's to you.

My plea to you is to learn to love what Jesus loves. He loves his bride more than any other thing on this earth. He loved her so much that he died for her. When husbands are called to love their wives, Scripture tells them to do so in the way that Christ loved the church (v. 25). He gave himself for her. One of the greatest ways you can love the bride of Christ is by joining a local church and then giving yourself to it. Follow through on what it means to be a member at that specific church.

CHURCH MEMBERSHIP

It begins by showing up.

After all, Sunday-morning church is a Saturday-night decision. Before you pull those covers over yourself and turn on that white noise for a good night's sleep, make the decision that you are going to be at church the next morning. This is a way you can love what Jesus loves—choose to do so. We decide to love.

If the church is going to reach the world for Jesus, we can't settle for "seldom is the new regular" when it comes to church attendance. Scale down for a moment from the big idea of the world being reached and think about your own community. If our faith gets the status of "seldom," what does that communicate to the lost in our community about what matters? Scale that down again and ask what it communicates to those immediately around you.

One might assert that just because you are seldom at church doesn't mean you are casual about your faith. But I wrote this book because, frankly, I'm afraid it does. A faith that is casual about church is a faith that is also casual. What do the children in your household think about the significance of the local church when once or twice a month maximum works for mom and dad? That seldom status is what they know as their normal. What was seldom for mom and dad will become "rare" for their children when they become adults, and "never" could be the status of their grandchildren. This must change quickly. The ramifications for the future of the local church demand it.

Being a pastor is an absolute privilege. I treasure the opportunity to shepherd the people of God through the office of pastor. Occasionally, I get asked what the hardest part is about my role. I'm not a big complainer about the difficulties of pastoring. There is far more good than bad. I get to see life change up close and have the best thing going (the local church) on my mind every day. It is the best job. But one difficulty is not talked about enough: how little of a priority the local church is for far too many professing Christians. One's favorite football team, workout routine, and book club generate more ownership of the calendar than the church in our current age. To state it again, something must give, or we will soon see a generation with no connection to the local church.

It is now normal for a Little League baseball practice to be on a Sunday morning or for people to go to their beach condo three weekends a month, seeing the lifeguard more regularly than they see their children's minister.

Why does everything else seem to come in the way of church? I long for a day when people can't do something else because they have church on Sunday morning. What would it take for you to be that kind of Christian? Does it feel like a radical thought that your weekend should consider the church rather than the church consider your weekend? It is time to start pushing back and asking why things are the way they are. This is not out of a spirit of condemnation, but rather a primary facet of the Christian faith that somehow became taboo to discuss. The good news is that it can change. And as cliché as it sounds, it really does happen one church member at a time. There is a tremendous opportunity, and now is the time for Christians to live out their church membership.

There are church members who love what Jesus loves and try to be there anytime the doors are open. That energizes and encourages a pastor in ways they may never know, but it also invigorates those around them and hopefully yields a bountiful harvest in their own lives. I know a family from our church with a son exceptionally talented at baseball. One of his select teams of elite players decided to have their weekly practice on Sunday mornings. All the parents agreed that it worked perfectly for their schedules, except for one family. It was, of course, that of the star kid on the team, who happens to be one of our church members. His dad raised his hand confused, asking why Sunday morning? Traditionally, that is reserved for church time. He told the other parents and coaches that anytime Sunday afternoon was great for them, but that his church meets on Sunday morning and his son would not be there if that was the decision. This family is invested in their son's baseball. He is on several teams, takes private lessons for his batting, and on Sunday morning this Christian family goes to church together more Sundays than seldom. On brand for today, the other parents busted out the legendary, "You don't have to go to church to be a Christian," and reminded the dad that they are all Christians too. He didn't argue otherwise, just repeated that they wouldn't be at practice if it was Sunday morning. That team now practices Sunday afternoons at 3:00 p.m. For this family, baseball matters, but church matters more.

While I don't expect anyone to be at church fifty-two Sundays a year (I know I never make perfect attendance, and I am the pastor), I do believe that to love what Jesus loves means *seldom* cannot be an accurate word to describe our involvement with the church. To know Christ is to love what he loves. Jesus loves his bride.

To love what Jesus loves means *seldom*
cannot be an accurate word to describe
our involvement with the church.

After showing up for church, we need to show our world Christ.

I call it showing up and then showing out. How we live for Christ outside the walls of the church is critical for church members. There is someone at your office whose entire opinion of the church where you are a member is linked to their knowledge of you. If you take your faith seriously outside the church, it brings credibility to your church, which is linked to the cause of Jesus Christ in your community.

Healthy church membership is an evangelism issue. It hurts the witness of the church when members either don't know Christ or live their lives like they haven't heard of him. You would be shocked to know how many people become members of local churches without anyone asking if they are believers in Jesus Christ. Ensuring one is regenerate and in the faith before joining your church is critical for the impact of your church in the community because it means that the members of this body are—without question—Christians. There is no false advertisement or ambiguity.

We often say, "Distinct lives point to a distinct God." This was the desire for God when it came to his people Israel. Surrounded by pagan nations, the Lord had a people for himself who were to stand out as a distinct people. Jesus, likewise, told his followers to "let your light shine before others" (Matt. 5:16). Our faith should be notably distinct from the secularism and gods of this world. Our faith is also linked to the specific church we claim, and our behaviors and attitudes reflect it to others. As representatives of Jesus Christ, we are representing his church, expressed locally, in our church membership.

When church membership matters, we can see three primary benefits:

1. *Membership in a local church benefits you.* How kind is the grace of God that the institution God calls us to give our lives to also benefits us personally! Our faith is designed to flourish in the context of the local church, and it will if we live our membership.

At our local church, we reserve a special moment in our worship service a few times a year for "parent commissioning." This is a special moment for members of our church who are parents of newborn babies. The families come before the church, and I ask the congregation to join in committing to pray for them. We pray for the marriage of the mother and father and the joys and struggles of parenthood, and we ask the Lord for the future salvation of the children. This, and many other moments like it, allow the members of a growing church to be seen and known by others who can then pursue relationship and fellowship together. Being a member of a local church means knowing other members are committed to praying for you and your family. My goal as a pastor is that every member of our church can be prayed with, prayed for, and personally discipled.

> Being a member of a local church means knowing other members are committed to praying for you and your family.

There is no other place I would rather be on a Sunday morning than at our church with our people. I have seen so many others come to believe and feel the same. Church is a weekly family reunion. I am sad for anyone who misses out on church membership while still professing Christ. They are missing out on an incredible blessing. May every Christian be a member of a local church. It is for your joy and flourishing as a follower of Jesus Christ.

2. Church membership benefits your witness for Christ. Coming alongside other believers who are facing the same tensions of being in the world but not of it, and who are striving to live faithfully for Christ, spurs us on together as disciples and encourages us in mission. I am going to be more prone to strive for faithful living when I know I have an entire church family who, by the Lord's grace, is choosing to do the same (Heb. 10:24). It is easy to grow weary and lose hope. Part of the function of the local church is to ensure that quitting is not a reality for our lives.

I recently had a conversation with my children regarding attending their siblings' sporting events and dance competitions. At times they moan and groan about having to go to a brother's football game or their sister's dance recital. I reminded them that as a family we are to be one another's biggest fans since we are on the same team. The same example can carry out in our spiritual family, as we seek to encourage one another to live on mission faithfully and fruitfully for the glory of God and advancement of his church.

3. Church membership benefits others. The local church needs you. Yes, you. We need your gifts, passions, prayers, and faithfulness. We even need your quirks and questions. The church needs your insights in a small-group Bible study and your consistent presence on a Sunday morning. One of the most others-focused acts you can do as a Christian is to live out your church membership. When you commit to a church, you are committing to a people. In fact, you are saying, "These are my people." The beauty of the church is that "your people" may be different from the folks you may have previously assumed would be the ones you would be in community with as a church. Nothing on earth can consistently and regularly bring people together from diverse backgrounds, situations, and stories than a local church. The church needs your place in that beautiful makeup of people.

> When you commit to a church, you
> are committing to a people.

Your church also needs you to give faithfully. Your church has a budget that goes to carrying out the Great Commission locally and across the world. Every dollar of that matters. Your church needs you to be part of that effort of cooperation in giving our financial resources, together, toward something Jesus ordained.

Your church needs you to serve. Your church needs you to be among the folks who say hello to the person who is at church every week alone and is trying to connect. We also need you to help others know they aren't the only ones who have ever had a hard day. Your sympathies, empathy, and compassionate grace are needed in the local church. You don't have to be extroverted or introverted, but simply part of the family. Living out your membership will not go unnoticed. God is pleased when his children are living the truth, and an entire church family of fellow members benefits because you are part of this mission.

So, if you are thinking, *Yes, I attended a membership class, I signed a form indicating a commitment to the church and desire to join the church, what now?* Now is the time to live out your membership. This means you do not live an independent faith, but rather one that is dependent on others to live the Christian life together. It means you have a certain set of beliefs that matter and that allow you to be in fellowship together with the truth as your foundation. Living your membership means you live generously, believing your financial resources are mission ammunition. It also means you are living your life knowing you represent far more than just yourself. You are, most importantly, being an ambassador for Christ, but also representing his church. Be countercultural even in today's church world by living out the conviction that the local church matters. Let "seldom is the new regular" end with you and (Lord willing) impact the next several generations of your family. God has a clear design for his people, and he loves you being a part of what he has made. The local church is the best thing going. Go all in. Please, be a church member.

Notes

Chapter 1

1. Jonathan Leeman, "The Church: Universal and Local," The Gospel Coalition, February 10, 2021, https://www.thegospelcoalition.org/essay/the-church-universal-and-local.

2. "New Data Suggests over 40 Percent of Self-Identified Evangelicals Attend Church Once a Year or Less," RELEVANT, April 8, 2021, https://relevantmagazine.com/faith/church/new-data-suggests-over-40-percent-of-self-identified-evangelicals-attend-church-once-a-year-or-less.

3. Nicholas Davis, "Why Should We Go to Church?," Nicholas Martin Davis, January 24, 2023, https://nicholasmartindavis.com/all/why-attend-church.

4. Jared C. Wilson, X, May 12, 2021, http://twitter.com/jaredcwilson/status/1392348688530411521?s=46.

Chapter 2

1. John R. W. Stott, *The Message of Ephesians* (Downers Grove, IL: IVP Academic, 2021), 9.

2. This is one of the core concepts of Gabe Lyons's book, *The Next Christians: Seven Ways You Can Live the Gospel and Restore the World* (Colorado Springs: Multnomah, 2012).

3. Jared C. Wilson, "Young People, Church Membership Isn't Optional," For the Church: Gospel-Centered Resources from Midwestern Seminary, May 1, 2023, https://ftc.co/resource-library/blog-entries/young-people-church-membership-isnt-optional.

4. Wilson, "Young People, Church Membership Isn't Optional."

5. Tim Keller, *Gospel in Life: Grace Changes Everything* (Grand Rapids: Zondervan, 2010), 58–71.

6. Richard Lints, "The Unity of the Church," The Gospel Coalition, accessed October 7, 2023, https://www.thegospelcoalition.org/essay/the-unity-of-the-church.

Chapter 3

1. Jonathan I. Griffiths, *Preaching in the New Testament* (Downers Grove, IL: InterVarsity Press, 2017), 128–29.

2. Timothy George, "Reformational Preaching," First Things, January 9, 2017, https://www.firstthings.com/web-exclusives/2017/01/reformational-preaching.

3. George, "Reformational Preaching."

4. Matt Morton, "Why Preaching Still Matters," DTS Voice, November 3, 2021, https://voice.dts.edu/article/why-preaching-matters/?.

Chapter 4

1. John Piper, "Why Do Christians Worship Together on Sundays?" Ask Pastor John, Desiring God, episode 790, February 9, 2016, https://www.desiringgod.org/interviews/why-do-christians-worship-together-on-sundays.

2. Piper, "Why Do Christians Worship Together on Sundays?".

3. Peter Mead, "What's the Big Deal with Worship?," Biblical Preaching, 2023, May 1, 2023, https://biblicalpreaching.net/2023/05/01/whats-the-big-deal-with-worship.

4. Quoted in Rod Dreher, *Live Not by Lies: A Manual for Christian Dissidents* (New York: Penguin, 2020), 185–86.

Chapter 5

1. James Montgomery Boice, *Psalms: Psalms 42–106* (Grand Rapids: Baker Publishing Group, 1996), 811.

2. Martin Luther, *Liturgy and Hymns*, ed. Ulrich S. Leupold Luther's Works, vol. 53 (Philadelphia: Fortress, 1965), 323.

3. Luther, *Liturgy and Hymns*.

4. Andrew Wilson, "The Unifying Power of Singing," The Gospel Coalition, September 1, 2021, https://www.thegospelcoalition.org/article/the-unifying-power-of-singing.

5. Rebecca Joy Stanborough, "10 Ways That Singing Benefits Your Health," Healthline, November 10, 2020, https://www.healthline.com/health/benefits-of-singing.

6. Jennie Pollock, "Together We Sing," Think, June 24, 2001, https://thinktheology.co.uk/blog/article/together_we_sing.

7. Pollock, "Together We Sing."

Chapter 6

1. Timothy J. Keller, *The New City Catechism: 52 Questions and Answers for Our Hearts and Minds* (Carol Stream, IL: Crossway, 2017), 105.

2. Gregg R. Allison, "The Ordinances of the Church," The Gospel Coalition, accessed October 8, 2023, https://www.thegospelcoalition.org/essay/the-ordinances-of-the-church.

3. Allison, "The Ordinances of the Church."

4. Allison, "The Ordinances of the Church."

5. Jonathan Griffiths, "The Lord's Supper," The Gospel Coalition, accessed October 7, 2023, https://www.thegospelcoalition.org/essay/the-lords-supper.

6. Griffiths, "The Lord's Supper."

Chapter 7

1. Stephen Wellum, "Water Baptism," The Gospel Coalition, accessed October 8, 2023, https://www.thegospelcoalition.org/essay/water-baptism.

2. Timothy J. Keller, *The New City Catechism: 52 Questions and Answers for Our Hearts and Minds* (Carol Stream, IL: Crossway, 2017), 107.

3. John Piper, "Why Was Jesus Baptized?" Ask Pastor John, Desiring God, Episode 773, January 15, 2016, https://www.desiringgod.org/interviews/why-was-jesus-baptized.

Chapter 8

1. A. W. Tozer, *The Pursuit of God* (Camp Hill, PA: Wingspread Publishers, 2008), 28.

2. Tom Schreiner, "7 Reasons Christians Are Not Required to Tithe," The Gospel Coalition, March 28, 2017, https://www.thegospelcoalition.org/article/7-reasons-christians-not-required-to-tithe.

Chapter 9

1. I first heard this in Gabe Lyons's book UnChristian, but it is also a main topic in his subsequent book, *The Next Christians: Seven Ways You Can Live the Gospel and Restore the World* (Colorado Springs: Multnomah, 2012), 67.

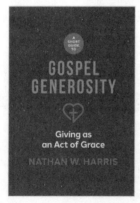
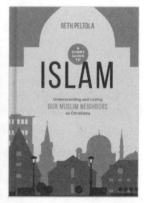